The Ridgeway

National Trail Companion

supported by

The
Countryside
Agency

1st edition published February 2000

© National Trails Office

ISBN 0-9535207-1-4

Edited by Jos Joslin & Alison Muldal

Photographs by Jos Joslin

Published by

National Trails Office

Cultural Services

Holton

Oxford OX33 1QQ

tel 01865 810224

fax 01865 810207

email mail@rway-tpath.demon.co.uk

website www.nationaltrails.gov.uk

Produced by Leap Frog Communications Ltd, Leeds

Designed by David Aldred

Cover photo:

Tan, who enjoyed The Ridgeway for the last ten of her
eleven years, on the Trail north of Tring Station.

Contents

I Introduction   5

II History   8

III Wildlife   9

IV Using The Ridgeway   11

V Finding Your Way   13

VI Publications   15

VII Useful Contacts   16

VIII Getting There   20

IX Respect the Countryside   21

X Emergency Contacts   22

XI Accommodation, Facilities & Services   24

Section 1 – Overton Hill to Uffington Castle   29

Section 2 – Uffington Castle to Streatley   47

Section 3 – Streatley to Chinnor   63

Section 4 – Chinnor to Ivinghoe Beacon   79

Index of Places   94

Notes   95

Looking south from Hackpen Hill, Wiltshire

Introduction

One hundred and thirty seven kilometres long, much of it following the ancient chalk ridge route used by prehistoric man and surrounded by numerous historic monuments, The Ridgeway offers the chance to get away from the bustle of life in this busy part of England. Perfect, but not too strenuous, for long distance use, this Trail is also ideal for day trips or less. The whole of The Ridgeway can be enjoyed by walkers with horseriders and cyclists able to use all of the western half as far as the River Thames at Streatley and short sections further east.

The Ridgeway

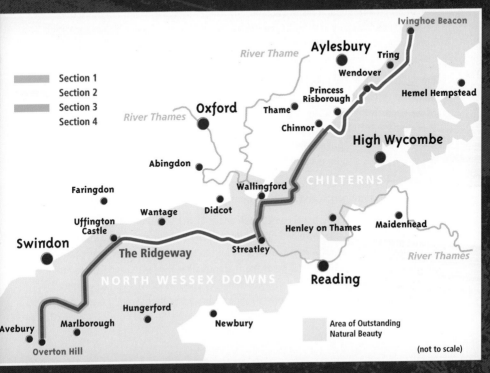

I INTRODUCTION

Welcome to this first Ridgeway Companion. It provides up-to-date practical information about accommodation, refreshments and many other facilities along the 137 km of National Trail. The Companion is designed to help with planning anything from a week's holiday to a short walk or ride.

The Companion is not a route guide: for detailed information about the Trail itself, The Ridgeway National Trail Guide by Neil Curtis (Aurum Press, 1999) is available from most book shops or from Amazon via the internet. Alternatively it can be mail ordered from the National Trails Office (see page 16 for details). The Companion complements the Trail Guide and, armed with a copy of each, it is hoped that anyone using The Ridgeway needn't require anything more. Enjoy your trip.

One of only 13 National Trails in England, The Ridgeway starts in the famous World Heritage Site of Avebury in Wiltshire and travels for 137 km steadily north east along the surprisingly remote scarp ridge of the downs, across the River Thames, and through the Chiltern Hills to finish in the Iron Age fort on top of Ivinghoe Beacon in Buckinghamshire.

The western half of The Ridgeway, as far as Streatley on the Thames, can be enjoyed by walkers, horseriders and cyclists, whereas only walkers can use the full extent of the eastern half. Despite its relative remoteness, public transport to The Ridgeway is pretty good, especially to the eastern half. Here there are several railway stations close to the Trail and an excellent bus network, and with a little planning many places along the western half can also be reached by bus or train or a combination of the two.

The Ridgeway passes through two distinctive landscapes; the open downland of the west and the more gentle and wooded countryside of the Chiltern Hills in the east.

In the west The Ridgeway travels as a broad ancient track along the open and fairly isolated top of the chalk downland ridge, often several kilometres from the nearest village. Here, to the south is rolling downland and to the north, at the bottom of the steep scarp slope, the wide expanse of the Thames Valley. The far-reaching views are dominated by the sky, the clouds and small clumps of beech woodland and all you may have for company is a solitary Skylark singing overhead or a hare chasing across an adjacent field.

In the past these downs were sheep grazed, but since the introduction of fertilisers earlier this century many areas have been ploughed and planted with crops. However sheep grazing does continue in places and, in others, a characteristic sight is immaculately managed grass tracks, the gallops used for training racehorses. The excellent turf of the downs makes this prime horse country but you need to be up early to see the strings of racehorses exercising.

At Goring on Thames The Ridgeway crosses the River Thames, and another of England's National Trails, the Thames Path, entering more intimate and less open countryside. It follows the bank of this famous river along a lovely 8 km rural stretch before heading eastwards into the Chiltern Hills. Mostly on narrower paths, the Trail passes through woodlands, many of them beech, over neatly cultivated fields and across chalk grassland nature reserves rich in wildflowers. In contrast to the western half, although its usually peaceful here, you're never far from pleasant small towns or attractive villages.

With the support of the Countryside Agency, The Ridgeway is managed to the highest standards necessary for one of the most important paths in the country by the local highway authorities with a small dedicated team of staff.

Wayland's Smithy, a New Stone Age long barrow 2 km southwest of Uffington Castle

7

II HISTORY

For thousands of years, at least 5,000 and maybe many more, people have walked or ridden The Ridgeway, be they drovers, traders, invaders or today's recreational visitors. As part of a prehistoric track once stretching about 400 km from the Dorset coast to the Wash on the Norfolk coast, The Ridgeway provided a route over the high ground for travellers which was less wooded and drier than routes through the springline villages below.

New Stone Age men, the first farmers in Britain, left the earliest remains. Their long barrows can be found at a few places both west and east of the River Thames. It was Bronze Age people from later times, around 2,000 BC, however, who dragged the huge sarsen stones from the surrounding hills and formed the dramatic Avebury Circle. There are many of their round burial barrows along the length of the National Trail.

Hill forts built during the Iron Age from about 500 BC until the Romans arrived in 43 AD are also found both sides of the Thames. These forts command the high ground and in several places they defended The Ridgeway against attack from the north.

In the Dark Ages The Ridgeway was a main route for the Saxons and Vikings who fought many battles during their advances into Wessex. In medieval times it was drovers driving livestock from Wales and the West Country to the Home Counties, not armies, who used The Ridgeway.

Until the Enclosure Acts of 1750 The Ridgeway was a broad band of tracks along the crest of the downs where travellers chose the driest or most convenient path. During Enclosures the exact course and width of The Ridgeway was defined by the building of earth banks and the planting of thorn hedges to prevent livestock straying into the newly cultivated fields.

In recent times use of The Ridgeway has changed greatly: farmers do still use much of it as an access route to their fields for tractors and other machinery but its main use is no longer utilitarian but recreational with walkers and riders out for exercise, pleasure and spiritual refreshment.

The grasslands which occur on the chalk of the downs and the Chiltern Hills are some of the most interesting habitats in England and some of the richest in terms of the number of plant species found. Chalk grassland has suffered from modern farming and much has disappeared under the plough. However those unimproved chalk grassland areas along The Ridgeway, especially the nature reserves east of the Thames, are well worth visiting where you'll find, amongst many other lovely plants, several types of orchid.

Another botanical treat in store for visitors during springtime is the carpet of bluebells in many of the woodlands in the Chiltern Hills, usually in the first couple of weeks of May.

For those keen on seeing birds, The Ridgeway should not disappoint you. A range of relatively common birds such as warblers and finches are found the length of The Ridgeway enjoying the food supply provided by the hedges lining the Trail. Skylarks, yellowhammers and corn buntings are particularly characteristic of the downland and although generally in decline in Britain are still numerous along The Ridgeway. The song of the corn bunting, likened to the sound of a jangle of keys, is the distinctive sound of the western half of The Ridgeway.

In colder months flocks of redwing and fieldfare, winter visitors from Scandinavia, are common and are usually seen feeding in the fields surrounding the Trail. However, most people will especially cherish the site of a red kite and you'll be unlucky if you don't see one in the Chiltern Hills. These magnificent birds of prey recognised by their forked tail were reintroduced to this area in the late 1980s and are now well established. In woodlands of this area too, woodpeckers and nuthatches may well be spotted.

Apart from the ubiquitous rabbit, hares and deer are the larger wild animals you may encounter. Hares are found in open countryside and are bigger than rabbits with longer ears and hind legs. They are solitary animals and most active at night, so late evening or early morning are the best times to see them. Two species of deer are found on The Ridgeway, roe and fallow with the former being the smaller and also living in smaller groups of just three or four animals. Both of these species are nocturnal and shy so, as for hares, being on The Ridgeway at dusk or dawn will give you the best chance of viewing them.

Southwest of Sparsholt

St Botolph's Swyncombe, an early Norman church dedicated to the patron saint of travellers

The Ridgeway provides excellent walking, cycling and horse riding opportunities although it is only walkers who can use the whole length of the Trail.

Cyclists and Horseriders

Riders, both cyclists and horseriders, can share The Ridgeway with walkers all the way from the start at Overton Hill near Avebury to Streatley on the River Thames, a distance of roughly 68 km. Once across the river the only long section of the Trail which can be ridden is the 13 km stretch which follows the Icknield Way through the Chilterns from Britwell Hill near Watlington to Wainhill on the Oxfordshire/ Buckinghamshire border. In other places The Ridgeway is a footpath and it is a trespass offence to ride on a footpath without the permission of the landowner.

However an alternative for riders is to join the Swan's Way long distance bridleway at Goring on Thames, just across the river from Streatley, and to follow this, mostly on The Ridgeway to Bledlow west of Princes Risborough (here the Swan's Way turns north). From Bledlow riders can pick up the Icknield Way Riders' Route which provides a good alternative to The Ridgeway for riders as far as Pitstone Hill, just a couple of kilometres from Ivinghoe Beacon. Unfortunately riders can't continue to Ivinghoe Beacon, the official end of the National Trail, since the route to it is on footpaths.

Vehicles

It's worth knowing, so that it doesn't come as a surprise to see a motorbike or four wheel drive, that vehicles can legally use most of the western half of The Ridgeway and a few sections east of the Thames. However recreational vehicles and motorcycles only comprise about 5% of the total usage of The Ridgeway with agricultural vehicles another 1%, so you're unlikely to meet too many vehicles.

Code of Respect

A Code of Respect has been operating on The Ridgeway for the last few years to encourage all users to act responsibly to conserve the Trail and to be aware and considerate of the rights of others. Details of the Code are shown on page 18 and you are asked to familiarise yourself with it before visiting The Ridgeway.

IV USING THE RIDGEWAY

Be prepared!

When venturing into the countryside it is wise to be prepared for the elements: even in summer, wind and rain can make a walk or ride cold and uncomfortable, so suitable warm and waterproof clothing should be worn or carried in a small rucksack. In the summer, especially on much of the western half of The Ridgeway which is exposed, it is also advisable to wear protection against the sun and to carry a water bottle since water points are relatively infrequent (see each section for information on these).

From April to the end of October most years The Ridgeway is usually dry with conditions on the whole good. There are, however, places where ruts have developed and care needs to be taken, so do wear strong, comfortable footwear. From November to March parts of The Ridgeway can become muddy making it difficult in places to walk or cycle - on the whole you'll find that the footpath sections are fine.

Dog Matters

If you are planning to undertake a long distance walk along The Ridgeway with your dog, you are advised to ensure it is fit before you start; on occasions walkers have had to abandon a walk because their dogs can't keep up!

Please also make sure your dog is under close control at all times to prevent it from disturbing livestock or wildlife. You are asked to keep your dog on a lead when you're in the few fields you'll encounter with livestock, although if you find that cattle seriously harass you because of the dog, it may be wise to let it off the lead.

Signing

The Ridgeway follows a series of well-signed public rights of way along which people have legal right of access.

An acorn, the symbol of Britain's National Trails, is used to guide your journey by marking the route in a variety of ways. It is used in conjunction with coloured arrows or the words 'footpath', 'bridleway' or 'byway' to indicate who can use a particular right of way.

The word 'footpath' and/or a yellow arrow indicates a path for use by walkers only and where, without the landowner's permission, it is illegal to cycle, ride a horse or drive a vehicle.

The word 'bridleway' and/or a blue arrow indicates a path which can be used by walkers, horseriders and cyclists but where, without the landowner's permission, it is illegal to drive any vehicle.

The word 'byway' and/or a red arrow indicates a right of way which can be legally used by walkers, horseriders, cyclists and motorists.

The Ridgeway is signposted where it crosses roads and other rights of way using mostly recycled plastic materials. Elsewhere, waymark discs with acorns and coloured arrows are used on gates and waymark posts.

Guides

'The Ridgeway National Trail Guide by Neil Curtis', Aurum Press, updated 1999 and costing £10.99 is the official guide with written route description and colour 1:25 000 maps.

Harveys have recently published 'Ridgeway', a detailed waterproof map at the scale of 1:40 000 of the entire National Trail which includes locations of facilities and services close to the Trail. It costs £7.95.

V FINDING YOUR WAY

Maps

It is usually a good idea to use maps when walking, particularly in unfamiliar areas. The National Trail Guide includes colour sections of all the appropriate 1:25 000 Ordnance Survey maps needed to follow The Ridgeway. Alternatively, for you to enjoy and interpret the wider landscape, you may wish to purchase your own Ordnance Survey maps.

The Landranger series (pink cover at 1:50 000 or 2 cm to 1 km) has all public rights of way, viewpoints, tourist information and selected places of interest marked on them. For the whole of The Ridgeway you will need:

173   Swindon and Devizes
174   Newbury and Wantage
175   Reading and Windsor
165   Aylesbury and Leighton Buzzard

The larger scale new Explorer series (orange cover at 1:25 000 or 4 cm to 1 km) has more detail including fence lines which can be very helpful when following rights of way, recreational routes and greater tourist information. For the whole of The Ridgeway you will need:

157   Marlborough and Savernake Forest
170   Abingdon, Wantage and Vale of White Horse
171   Chiltern Hills West
181   Chiltern Hills North

For those people with the old Pathfinder series (green cover at 1:25 0000 or 4 cm to 1 km) for the whole of the Trail you will need:

1185 (SU06/16)   Devizes and Marlborough
1169 (SU07/17)   Marlborough Downs
1170 (SU27/37)   Lambourn and Aldbourne
1154 (SU28/38)   Lambourn Downs
1155 (SU48/58)   Wantage (East) and Didcot (South)
1156 (SU68/78)   Henley-on-Thames and Wallingford
1137 (SU69/79)   Watlington and Stokenchurch
1117 (SP60/70)   Thame
1118 (SP80/90)   Chesham and Wendover
1094 (SP81/91)   Aylesbury and Tring

Publications About The Ridgeway

Below is a selection of publications about The Ridgeway:

The Ridgeway National Trail Guide by Neil Curtis, Aurum Press, updated 1999 - the official guide with written route description and colour 1:25 000 maps. Available from the National Trails Office.

Ridgeway, Harvey Maps, 1999 - 1:40 000 scale waterproof map of the entire route of The Ridgeway including information on a range of facilities along the Trail. Available from the National Trails Office.

Exploring the Ridgeway by Alan Charles, Countryside Books, 1994 (due to be revised in 2000) - based on 14 circular walks covering the whole length of The Ridgeway.

The Oldest Road - an Exploration of the Ridgeway by J R L Anderson with photographs by Fay Godwin, Wildwood House, 1975. Paperback edition by Whittet Books, 1992.

The Ridgeway - a map guide by Footprint, revised edition 1994.

The Mountain Biker's Guide to the Ridgeway by Andy Bull and Frank Barrett, Stanley Paul & Co, 1991.

Ridgeway Routes Pack - leaflets describing circular and other walks from The Ridgeway. Available from the National Trails Office.

Ridgeway Circular Riding Routes Pack - leaflets describing circular rides from The Ridgeway. Available from the National Trails Office.

Let's Hear it for The Ridgeway! by Elizabeth Newbery - a family activity book full of ideas and information on things to do and see on and close to The Ridgeway. Available from the National Trails Office.

Ridgeway Public Transport Leaflet - details of bus and train services for the whole Trail. Free from the National Trails Office.

Events Programme - a range of guided events around The Ridgeway. Free from the National Trails Office.

VII USEFUL CONTACTS

The Ridgeway Manager

Jos Joslin, National Trails Office, Cultural Services, Holton, Oxford OX33 1QQ. Telephone 01865 810224. Fax 01865 810207. Email: mail@rway-tpath.demon.co.uk

Highway Authorities responsible for public rights of way

Buckinghamshire County Council, Environmental Services Dept, County Hall, Walton Street, Aylesbury HP20 1UY. Telephone 01296 395000

Hertfordshire County Council, Planning and Environment, County Hall, Hertford SG13 8DN. Telephone 01992 555555

Oxfordshire County Council, Countryside Service, Cultural Services, Holton, Oxford OX33 1QQ. Telephone 01865 810226

Swindon Borough Council, Borough Engineer's Dept, Premier House, Station Road, Swindon SN1 1TZ. Telephone 01793 463000

West Berkshire Council, Countryside and Environment, Faraday Road, Newbury RG14 2AF. Telephone 01635 42400

Wiltshire County Council, Dept of Environmental Services, County Hall, Trowbridge, Wilts BA14 8JD. Telephone 01225 713000

Agency responsible for National Trails

Countryside Agency, South East and London Region, Dacre House, 19 Dacre Street, London SW1H 0DH. Telephone 0207 3402900

Organisations for walkers

Backpackers Club, c/o Jim & Maggie Beed, 49 Lyndhurst Road, Exmouth, Devon EX8 3DS. Telephone 01395 265159

Long Distance Walkers Association, c/o Brian Smith, 10 Temple Park Close, Leeds, W Yorks LS15 0JJ. Tel (0113) 2642205

Oxford Fieldpaths Society, c/o Mr D Godfrey, 23 Hawkswell House, Hawkswell Gardens, Oxford OX2 7EX. Tel (01865) 514082

Ramblers Association,1-5 Wandsworth Road, London SW8 2XX. Telephone 0207 3398500

Code of Respect

To respect this National Trail so that it can be enjoyed by all, please . . .

Act responsibly to conserve The Ridgeway

Be aware and considerate of the rights of others

FOR RECREATION YOU CAN

Use all The Ridgeway

Use all except footpath sections

Use all except footpath and bridleway sections

CODE OF RESPECT – YOU SHOULD

Understand that others have legitimate access to many sections

Spread the message about responsible care

Follow the Country Code

Limit your use when the surface is vulnerable during and after wet weather

Avoid using The Ridgeway if you can find or develop another route

Keep to well-used parts of the track to prevent damage to the whole width

Continue to help by reinstating the surface where possible

Make sure you and your vehicle are fully road-legal

Make sure your bicycle is roadworthy

Drive at a quiet and careful speed with no more than 4 wheeled vehicles or 8 motorcycles in any one group

Ride at a safe and controlled pace

Help other users and make your own visit more enjoyable by using The Ridgeway when it is less busy

Warn walkers of your approach and pass carefully

Warn walkers and horseriders of your approach and give way to them

Give way to horseriders

Watch out for and respect temporary voluntary restraint signs and report registration numbers of those who break codes to LARA (Motoring Organisations' Land Access & Recreation Association). Tel: 01543 467218

KEY

walker

cyclist

horserider

carriage driver

motorcyclist

driver - recreational four wheeled vehicle

driver - agricultural vehicle

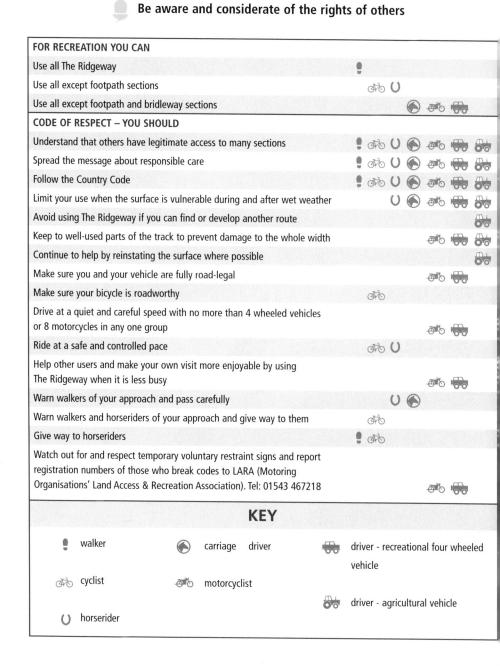

Organisations for cyclists

British Cycling Federation, National Cycling Centre, Stuart Street, Manchester M11 4DQ. Telephone 0161 2302301

Cyclists Touring Club (Off-Road), Cotterell House, 69 Meadrow, Godalming, Surrey GU7 3HS. Telephone 01483 417217

Sustrans, 33 King Street, Bristol BS1 4DZ. Telephone 0117 9268893

Organisations for horseriders

British Horse Society, Stoneleigh Deer Park, Kenilworth, Warwicks CV8 2XZ. Telephone 01926 707700

Byways & Bridleways Trust, PO Box 117, Newcastle upon Tyne NE3 5YT. Telephone 0191 2364086

Endurance Horse & Pony Society, c/o Mrs Wendy Dunham, Tudor Nurserie, Chalk Pit Lane, Wool, Wareham BH20 6DW. Telephone 01929 462316

Wiltshire Bridleways Association, Follyfield, Maddington Street, Shrewton, Salisbury, Wilts SP3 4JL. Telephone 01980 620577

Other organisations

Berkshire, Buckinghamshire & Oxfordshire Wildlife Trust, The Lodge, 1 Armstrong Road, Littlemore, Oxford OX4 4XT. Telephone 01865 775476

Chiltern Society, The White Hill Centre, White Hill, Chesham, HP5 1AG. Telephone 01494 771250

Friends of the Ridgeway, c/o Mr Peter Gould, 18 Hampton Park, Bristol BS6 6LH.

Herts & Middlesex Wildlife Trust, Grebe House, St Michael's Street, St Albans AL3 4SN. Telephone 01727 858901

Wiltshire Wildlife Trust, Elm Tree Court, Long Street, Devizes, SN10 1NJ. Telephone 01380 725670

VIII GETTING THERE

Getting to The Ridgeway by public transport is fairly easy, particularly the eastern half of the Trail, and a useful map-based leaflet showing relevant public transport routes is available free from the National Trails Office (see page 16 for details).

Alternatively, telephone numbers and websites to find out more about public transport to the Trail are listed below:

- National Rail (all sections)   24 hours a day 0345 484950
  www.railtrack.co.uk

- Section One   Wiltshire County Council
  0345 090899

  Swindon Borough Council
  01793 466214

  Oxfordshire County Council
  01865 810405

- Section Two   Oxfordshire County Council
  01865 810405

  West Berkshire Council
  0118 9015900

- Section Three   Oxfordshire County Council
  01865 810405

- Section Four   Oxfordshire County Council
  01865 810405

  Buckinghamshire County Council
  0345 382000

  Hertfordshire County Council
  0345 244344

Information about taxi services is included in each of the four sections.

Those wishing to travel to The Ridgeway by car are asked to park considerately if parking in villages on or close to the Trail. Other places to park are listed within each section.

- Enjoy the countryside, but remember that most of The Ridgeway crosses private farmland and estates which are living and working landscapes.

- Always keep to the Trail to avoid trespass and use gates and stiles to negotiate fences and hedges.

- Crops and animals are the farmer's livelihood - please leave them alone.

- To avoid injury or distress to farm animals and wildlife, keep your dogs under close control at all times - preferably on a lead through fields with farm animals (NB if you are concerned that cattle are harassing you, it may be safer to let your dog off the lead).

- Remember to leave things as they are - fasten those gates you find closed. Straying farm animals can cause damage and inconvenience.

- Please take your litter home, otherwise it can injure people and animals and looks unsightly.

- Guard against all risk of fires especially in dry weather.

- Take special care on country roads and, if travelling by car, park sensibly so as not to obstruct others or gateways.

From Lodge Hill, southwest of Princes Risborough

X EMERGENCY CONTACTS

In emergency dial 999 and ask for the service required.

Police

To contact local police stations, telephone the number relevant to the section/county you are in and ask to be put through to the nearest police station.

Section	County	Tel Number
1	Wiltshire	01793 528111
	Oxfordshire	01865 846000
2	Oxfordshire & Berkshire	01865 846000
3	Oxfordshire	01865 846000
4	Oxfordshire & Buckinghamshire	01865 846000
	Hertfordshire	01707 354200

Grim's Ditch east of Wallingford during Spring

Hospitals

The following hospitals with casualty departments are located in the places shown below. The telephone numbers given are the hospital switchboard; ask to be put through to Accident and Emergency Reception.

◆ Full 24-hour emergency service

▼ Minor injuries only, 24-hour service

▲ Minor injuries only, NOT 24-hour service

Section	Town	Telephone No	Address
1	▼ Devizes	01380 723511	Devizes Community Hospital, Commercial Road, Devizes
	▲ Marlborough	01672 516631	Savernake Hospital, London Road, Marlborough (daily 8am-10pm)
	◆ Swindon	01793 536231	Princess Margaret Hospital, Okus Road, Swindon
2	▼ Wantage	01235 403801	Wantage Community Hospital, Garston Lane, Wantage
	▲ Didcot	01235 517900	Didcot Hospital, Wantage Road, Didcot (weekdays 6pm - 8am, weekends/bank hols 24 hrs)
3	▼ Wallingford	01491 835533	Wallingford Community Hospital, Reading Road, Wallingford
4	◆ Aylesbury	01296 315000	Stoke Mandeville Hospital, Mandeville Road, Aylesbury

XI ACCOMMODATION, FACILITIES & SERVICES

This booklet gives details of the settlements, accommodation, eating places, shops, attractions and other facilities along The Ridgeway. They are listed in geographic order from Overton Hill to Ivinghoe Beacon.

If you fail to find accommodation using this guide please contact the Tourist Information Centres listed near the beginning of each section which may be able to provide other addresses.

The Ridgeway is divided into four sections as indicated on the map on page 5. At the start of each section is a map showing the settlements close to the Trail within that section. These maps are meant only as a guide and you are recommended to use this Companion in conjunction with The Ridgeway National Trail Guide or maps.

You are strongly advised to book accommodation in advance, and during summer as early as possible. Whilst booking, do check prices since those quoted here are usually the minimum charged.

For those who would like to enjoy more than a day on The Ridgeway without having to carry all their possessions, quite a few accommodation providers have indicated whether they are willing to transport the luggage you don't need during the day to your next night's accommodation. The fee charged for this service needs to be discussed and agreed at the time of the booking. Accommodation providers have also indicated if they are willing to collect you from The Ridgeway and deliver you back after your stay.

All the information within this Companion is as accurate as possible. Inclusion of accommodation does not constitute a recommendation although it is indicated in the details whether an establishment has a recognised grade awarded to it. If you have any comments or notice any errors, please write to Jos Joslin the National Trails Officer (page 16).

Camping on The Ridgeway

The situation regarding camping on The Ridgeway is, in theory, clear enough; The Ridgeway is privately owned and the public right of way along it is for passage only, not for stopping and camping.

In practice, however, most landowners do not object if a tent is pitched on The Ridgeway for a night and disappears the next morning as long as no litter is left, no damage done, nor camp fires lit. Do not camp in adjoining fields, woods or gallops without prior permission from the landowner.

Key to Symbols for Settlements

Any comments relate to preceding icon.

	map grid reference (see start of each section for relevant maps)
	shortest walking distance from The Ridgeway
	telephone
	toilets
	pub (usually open lunchtimes 11am-3pm then evenings 6pm-11pm)
✕	bar meals in pub
✉	post office (usual opening hours 9am-5.30pm weekdays; closed 12.30pm Sat)
	general store (usual opening hours daily 9am-5.30pm Mon-Sat)
	cafe/tea shop
	restaurant
	food take-away

opening hours of services relate to the preceding symbol
S M T W T F S

For example: open all day open afternoon/evening

  closed all day open morning/lunchtime

£	bank (usually open daily 9.30am-4.30pm Mon-Fri)
	cash machine available including outside bank opening hours
	Tourist Information Centre
☆	tourist attraction

XI ACCOMMODATION, FACILITIES & SERVICES

Key to Symbols for Accommodation

Type of accommodation (symbols in margins)

A symbol in the margin indicates whether camping, youth hostel, self-catering or horse accommodation is available at that address - which may be in addition to bed and breakfast accommodation.

 youth hostel

 camping

 self-catering accommodation

 grazing or stabling for horses

Accommodation symbols

The number and price following the symbols for rooms gives the number and price of that type of room available. The same applies to tent/caravan pitches and stabling/grazing for horses. Prices quoted for rooms are the minimum price per room per night for bed and breakfast. The price for single occupancy of double, twin or family rooms is given in brackets eg **(£22.00)**. The price for self-catering accommodation is the minimum charged per week.

🛏	double room	🐕	dogs allowed by arrangement
🛏	twin room	👫	children welcome
🛏	family room	🚭	no smoking allowed in bedrooms
🛏	single room	♿	wheelchair access
V	caters for vegetarians	**DRY**	clothes/boots drying facilities
🍎	packed lunches available	🚲	cycle storage
●	evening meals available at accommodation or locally	🚗	transport to and from Trail by arrangement

luggage transported to next overnight stop by arrangement		hot water	
English Tourism Council grade for B&Bs, guest houses, inns		cold water	
English Tourism Council grade for hotels		toilets	
tent pitches		laundry facilities	
caravan pitches		site shop	
showers		stables	
		grazing for horses	
		special feature/comment	

Perch & Pike, South Stoke

Uffington Castle

Avebury Stone Circle

Section 1

Overton Hill to Uffington Castle

Probably the most remote section of The Ridgeway, this 35 km stretch of broad track runs along the ridge of chalk downland in Wiltshire and Oxfordshire. It passes through an immensely rich area of archaeology and past the only pub directly on the western half of the Trail!

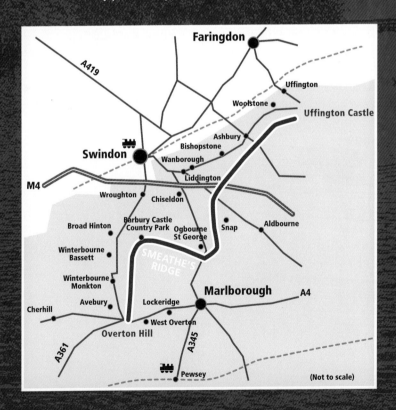

Faringdon
A419
Uffington
Woolstone
Uffington Castle
Ashbury
Bishopstone
Swindon
Wanborough
M4
Liddington
Wroughton
Chiseldon
Barbury Castle
Country Park
Broad Hinton
Ogbourne
St George
Snap
Aldbourne
Winterbourne
Bassett
SMEATHE'S
RIDGE
Winterbourne
Monkton
Marlborough
A4
Cherhill
Avebury
Lockeridge
West Overton
Overton Hill
A361
A345
Pewsey
(Not to scale)

A Taster

In places you can feel on top of the world with undulating downland and dry valleys or combes to the south and the Thames Valley stretching away northwards to the Cotswolds in the far distance. A characteristic sight from Overton Hill to Barbury Castle is small clumps of beech woodland planted by the Victorians as landscape features and to give sheep some shelter. Some clumps are even planted on top of Bronze Age round barrows, frowned upon today because of the damage tree roots do to ancient monuments.

The countryside is a mixture of arable land, which changes colour with the seasons, and areas of sheep or cattle grazed grassland. Some of the best views are from Smeathe's Ridge between Barbury Castle and Ogbourne St George.

The villages of Ogbourne St George in the valley of the River Og and those at the foot of the downs such as Bishopstone, Ashbury and Woolstone contain many lovely cottages some of them built out of blocks of chalk with thatched roofs.

This section includes a crossing by bridge of the M4, but the motorway only intrudes upon your journey for a short while and is soon lost as you climb away from it.

Bishopstone

History

This section starts in what is probably the richest area of archaeology in Britain, the World Heritage Site of Avebury. Within 2 km of the start at Overton Hill you can reach the Avebury Stone Circle, Silbury Hill (the largest man-made mound in Europe constructed by Stone Age people using antler picks and shovels made from the shoulder blades of oxen), West Kennett long barrow, the Sanctuary, the Stone Avenue and Fyfield Down National Nature Reserve littered with sarsen stones.

Travelling north, below you at Hackpen Hill you pass the first of the hill figures cut into the chalk which are scattered along the length of The Ridgeway. The Hackpen White Horse was created in 1838 by a local parish clerk. A little further on you reach the first of three Iron Age forts found in this section, Barbury Castle. Unlike the other two, Liddington Castle and Uffington Castle, both of which The Ridgeway skirts, you pass right through the centre of this fort.

Just northeast of Ogbourne St George to the east of The Ridgeway lies the deserted village of Snap abandoned early this century as a result of agricultural depression. With records dating from 1268, by 1841 Snap was a thriving if small farming community of 47 people. However, cheap corn from America in the 1870s caused the rapid decline in the population and the village's final demise. Today just low piles of sarsen rubble marking the site of cottages remain visible during winter months.

Before you reach Uffington Castle, away to the south is the delightful 17th century Ashdown House set in a tremendous remote dry valley location and the fine Wayland's Smithy long barrow just 50 m north of your route.

Maps

Landranger maps	173	Swindon and Devizes
	174	Newbury and Wantage
Explorer maps	157	Marlborough and Savernake Forest
	170	Abingdon, Wantage and Vale of White Horse
Pathfinder maps	1185 (SU06/16)	Devizes and Marlborough
	1169 (SU07/17)	Marlborough Downs
	1170 (SU27/37)	Lambourn & Aldbourne
	1154 (SU28/38)	Lambourn Downs

Public Transport Information

National Rail all sections   24 hours a day 0345 484950
       www.railtrack.co.uk
Wiltshire County Council   0345 090899
Swindon Borough Council   01793 466214
Oxfordshire County Council   01865 810405

Car Parking

The following are places close to or on The Ridgeway, other than villages or towns, with parking for vehicles - at some only for a few. Unfortunately theft from vehicles parked in the countryside does occasionally occur, so please leave valuables at home.

Place	Map Grid Reference
On Ridgeway at the start at Overton Hill, on north side of A4, 7 km west of Marlborough	SU 119681
On Ridgeway at Hackpen Hill on minor road between Marlborough and Broad Hinton, 3 km east of Broad Hinton	SU 129747
On Ridgeway at Barbury Castle Country Park, 8 km south of Swindon signed from Wroughton and Chiseldon	SU 157762
On Ridgeway at Fox Hill near Wanborough, 200m northeast of Shepherds Rest pub on road to Hinton Parva	SU 233814
On Ridgeway 1 km south of Ashbury on B4000	SU 274844
National Trust car park for Uffington White Horse, south off B4507	SU 293866

Taxis

Place	Name	Telephone Number
Pewsey	Maverick Taxis	0831 336624
Marlborough	Marlborough Radio Cars	01672 511088
	Marlborough Taxis	01672 512786
	Merlin Car Service	01672 513890
	Arrow Private Hire	01672 515567
Swindon	Ambassador Radio Cars	01793 535354
	A1 Radio Cars	01793 513333
	Abbey Radio Cars	01793 611111
	Swindon Taxi Company	01793 430999
	Millennium Radio Cars	01793 610000
Shrivenham	Shrivenham Private Car Hire	01793 782934

Water Taps

- with troughs for animals

Place	Map Grid Reference
Barbury Castle Country Park (at the bungalow)	SU 158760
Elm Tree Cottage, Southend	SU 198734
• Shepherds Rest Pub, Fox Hill	SU 232813
• Idstone Barn, Ashbury	SU 263835

Toilets

Place	Map Grid Reference
Barbury Castle Country Park	SU 155762
Shepherds Rest Pub, Fox Hill (patrons only)	SU 232813

Police

Wiltshire	01793 528111
Oxfordshire	01865 846000

Hospitals

Place	Telephone Number	Address
Devizes	01380 723511	Devizes Community Hospital, Commercial Road, Devizes
Marlborough	01672 516631	Savernake Hospital, London Road, Marlborough (daily 8am-10pm)
Swindon	01793 536231	Princess Margaret Hospital, Okus Road, Swindon

Vets

Place	Name	Telephone Number
Marlborough	Holden & Reader	01672 512043
	Hayward & Sercombe	01672 514875
Wroughton	Archway	01793 812542
Swindon	Drove Veterinary Hospital	01793 522483
	Stratton Veterinary Centre	01793 832461
	Lawn Veterinary Hospital	01793 644422
Lambourn	Ridgeway Group	01488 71002
Faringdon	Danetree	01367 242777
	Elms Surgery	01367 242416

Farriers

Place	Name	Telephone Number
Marlborough	Baker	01672 514013
Aldbourne	Racing Farriers	01672 540812
Swindon	P J Groom	01793 644123
Wroughton	P A Groom	01793 814185
Shrivenham	T P Morrissey	01793 783581
Lambourn	Alderton	01488 72583
	Charles	01488 71310 or 0831 595073
	Pickford	01488 72613

Saddlers

Place	Name	Telephone Number
Marlborough	Frederick Chandler	01672 512633
Purton (near Swindon)	Elmgrove Saddlery	01793 770613
Highworth	The Saddlery	01793 766660
Lambourn	Wicks	01488 71766
Faringdon	S and J M Cooper	01367 240517

Mountain Bike Hire

Place	Name	Telephone Number
Swindon	Swindon Cycles	01793 700105
	Express Cycles	0800 018 29253
Barbury Castle	Barbury Bike Hire	01793 845346 or 0831 139634

Bike Repairs

Place	Name	Telephone Number
Swindon	Mitchell Cycles	01793 523306
	Swindon Cycles	01793 700105
	Bike Doctor	01793 874873
	Express Cycles	0800 01829253
	Total Fitness	01793 644185

Racehorses during morning exercise

Cottage in Ashbury

Tourist Information Centres

★ offers accommodation booking service

Place	Address/Opening Hours
Avebury	Portacabin, The Great Barn, Avebury, SN8 1RF Tel: 01672 539425
★ Marlborough	George Lane Car Park, Marlborough SN8 1EE, Tel/Fax: 01672 513989
	Opening hours: Summer (Apr-Oct) Mon-Sat 10:00-17:00, Sun 10:30-16:30 Winter (Nov-Mar) Mon-Sat 10:00-16:30
★ Swindon	37 Regent Street, Swindon SN1 1JL Tel: 01793 530328 Fax: 01793 434031
	Opening hours: All year: Mon-Sat 09:30-17:30
★ Faringdon	7a Market Place, Faringdon SN7 7HL Tel/Fax: 01367 242191
	Opening hours: Summer (1 Apr-31 Oct) Mon-Fri 10:00-13:00, 13:30-17:00, Sat 10:00-13:00 Winter (1 Nov-31 Mar) Mon-Sat 10:00-13:00

Ashdown House 4 km south of Ashbury

PEWSEY

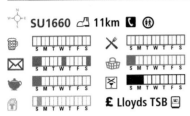 SU1660 🥾 11km 📞 ⓐ

🍺	S M T W T F S
×	S M T W T F S
✉	S M T W T F S
🧺	S M T W T F S
☕	S M T W T F S
🍴	S M T W T F S
⛽	S M T W T F S

£ Lloyds TSB 🖾
Co-operative Bank 🖾

Huntlys Farm   *all year*

Mrs M Andrews
Huntlys Farm, Manningford Abbotts,
PEWSEY SN9 6HZ
☎ 01672 563663 **Fax:** 01672 851249

🛏 1 🛏 1 🛏 1 £34.00 (£22.00)
V 🚴 🚫 🔳 🏃 over 6 years 🚭 **DRY**
🚲 🚗 👣 ◆◆

Ⓢ 3 £6.00 Ⓖ 3 £5.00

MARLBOROUGH

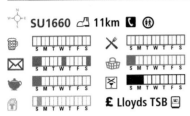 SU1969 🥾 7km Market town
with range of services 🛈

West View B&B   *all year*

Mrs M Trevelyan-Hall
West View B&B, Barnfield,
MARLBOROUGH SN8 2AX
☎ 01672 515583 **Mob:** 0771 216 5258
Fax: 01672 515583
Email: maggiestewart@euphony.net

🛏 2 £40.00 (£30.00) V 🚴 🚫 🔳
👫 🚭 ♿ **DRY** 🚲 👣 ◆◆◆

LOCKERIDGE

SU1467 🥾 3km 📞

S M T W T F S		S M T W T F S

The Taffrail   closed Dec

Mrs J Spencer
The Taffrail, Back Lane, Lockeridge,
MARLBOROUGH SN8 4ED
☎ 01672 861266 **Fax:** 01672 861266

🛏 1 🛏 1 £35.00
🛏 1 £20.00 (£20.00)

WEST OVERTON

SU1368 🥾 1km 📞

S M T W T F S		S M T W T F S
S M T W T F S		S M T W T F S

Cairncot   all year

Mrs R Leigh
Cairncot, West Overton, MARLBOROUGH
SN8 4ER
☎ 01672 861617 **Mob:** 0779 860 3455

🛏 1 £40.00 🛏 1 £20.00 (£30.00)

V 🔥 🚫 📷 ✳ 🚭 **DRY** 🚲 🧗
♦♦♦

CHERHILL

SU0370 🥾 9.5km 📞

S M T W T F S		S M T W T F S
S M T W T F S		

Poachers Croft   all year

Mrs O Trafford
Poachers Croft, Cherhill, CALNE SN11
8XY
☎ 01249 812587

🛏 1 🛏 1 🛏 1 £37.50 (£25.00)

V 🔥 🚫 📷 ✳ ♿ **DRY** 🚲 🚗
♦♦♦

Barbury Castle from the west

AVEBURY

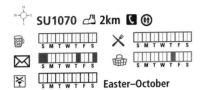

SU1070 🥾 2km 📞 ⊗

Easter–October

Nov, Feb, March

ℹ️ ☆ Avebury Stone Circle and Silbury Hill; Alexander Keiller Museum (Tel: 01672 539250)

Bannings Yard   *closed Nov–Easter*

Ms G Brunskill
Bannings Yard, Bray Street, Avebury,
MARLBOROUGH SN8 1RA
☎ 01672 539448 **Fax:** 01672 539692

🛏 1 £45.00 (£38.00) **V** 🚫 ⚥ ⊗
♿ **DRY** 🚲

Manor Farm   *closed Nov–Mar*

Mrs J Butler
Manor Farm, Avebury Trusloe,
MARLBOROUGH SN8 1QY
☎ 01672 539243 **Fax:** 01672 539230

🛏 1 £45.00 (£36.00)

V 🚫 ⊗ ♦♦♦

WINTERBOURNE MONKTON

SU1072 🥾 3km 📞

The New Inn   *all year*

Mrs D Murrin
The New Inn, Winterbourne Monkton,
SWINDON SN4 9NW
☎ 01672 539240 **Fax:** 01672 539150

🛏 2 🛏 3 £45.00 (£30.00) **V** 🧺
🚫 📺 ⚥ ⊗ **DRY** 🚲 🚗 🐕
♦♦♦

WINTERBOURNE BASSETT

SU1075 🥾 3km 📞

BROAD HINTON

SU1076 🥾 3km 📞

BARBURY CASTLE

SU1576 🥾 on The Ridgeway

🫖 ⬜⬜⬜⬜⬜⬜⬜ 📞 ♿ ☆ Barbury
S M T W T F S
Castle Country Park (Tel: 01793 771419)

🛖 Frog 'n' Spoon   *all year*

Mrs L Simpson
Frog 'n' Spoon, Ridgeway Farm, Barbury
Castle Country Park, Wroughton,
SWINDON SN4 0QH
☎ 01793 845346 **Fax:** 01793 845346
Mob: 0831 139634

🛖 20 £5.00 V 🔥 ⊘ 🎒 ⛺ ♿ 🚲
🔥 🔥 ♿ 📷

WROUGHTON

SU1480 🥾 4km 📞 ♿

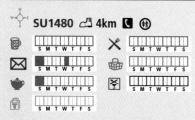

☆ Science Museum (Tel: 01793 814466)

SWINDON

SU1583 🥾 9km Large town
with range of services 🛈
☆ Oasis Leisure Centre (Tel: 01793
445400); Swindon Museum & Art Gallery
(Tel: 01793 466556); Great Western
Railway Museum and Railway Village
Museum (Tel: 01793 466555); Coate Water
Country Park (Tel: 01793 490150)

OGBOURNE ST GEORGE

SU2074 🥾 1km 📞

Foxlynch   *all year* 🛖

Mr G Edwins
Foxlynch, Bytham Road, Ogbourne St
George, MARLBOROUGH SN8 1TD
☎ 01672 841307

🛏 1 (£15.00) 🔥 ⊘ 🎒 ⛺ **DRY**
🚲 🚗 🐾 🍴 family bunk room in
stable block

🛖 4 £4.00 🚐 2 £5.00 📖 🔥 🔥 ♿

Ⓢ 4 £8.00

Parklands Hotel *all year*

Mr M Bentley
Parklands Hotel, High Street, Ogbourne St
George, MARLBOROUGH SN8 1SL
☎ 01672 841555 **Fax:** 01672 841533
Email: m.a.r.b@btinternet.com

🛏 2 🛏 6 £60.00
🛏 2 £30.00 (£50.00)

The Old Crown *all year*

Mr & Mrs M Shaw
The Old Crown, Marlborough Road,
Ogbourne St George, MARLBOROUGH
SN8 1SQ
☎ 01672 841445 **Email:**
TheInnwiththeWell@compuserve.com

🛏 2 🛏 2 🛏 1 £35.00 (£25.00)

CHISELDON

LIDDINGTON

Street House Farm *all year*

Mrs E Dixon
Street House Farm, Liddington, SWINDON
SN4 0HD
☎ 01793 790243

🛏 1 🛏 1 £36.00 (£20.00)

V 🚶 ● ✚ ⊘ **DRY** 🚲 🚗 🚶

WANBOROUGH

SU2182 👢 2km 📞

Iris Cottage *closed Xmas*

Mrs J Rosier
Iris Cottage, Burycroft, Lower
Wanborough, SWINDON SN4 0AP
☎ 01793 790591

🛏 1 £40.00 🛏 2 £20.00 (£20.00)

🚶 ● ⊘ **DRY** 🚲 🚗

Cheney Thatch

Bishopstone, Swindon, Wiltshire ☎ 01793 790508

16th Century stone thatched cottage in unique peaceful setting. Trout stream through garden, summer marquee. Heated outdoor swimming pool. Footpath to Ridgeway from garden gate.

The Shepherds Rest *open all year*

Mr H Kayne
The Shepherds Rest, Foxhill,
Wanborough, SWINDON SN4 0DR
☎ 01793 790266 **Fax:** 01793 790353
Email: sheprest@FSBDial.co.uk

⚑ 6 £3.00 🛏 🚰 🚰 ⚙

V 🥾 🚱 🎒 ♿ **DRY** 🥾 Offers a 3-day camping, meals, transport package.

BISHOPSTONE

 SU2483 ⛺ 1km 📞

S M T W T F S ✕
S M T W T F S

Cheney Thatch *closed Xmas*

Mrs R Boot
Cheney Thatch, Oxon Lane, Bishopstone,
SWINDON SN6 8PS
☎ 01793 790508

🛏 2 £40.00 (£25.00) **V** 🥾 🚱 👫
🚫 **DRY** 🚲 🚗 🐾 🥾 Garden marquee with 4 camp beds also available at £12.50/person/night

Prebendal Farm — closed Dec, Jan

Mrs J Selbourne
Prebendal Farm, Bishopstone, SWINDON
SN6 8PT
☎ 01793 790485 **Fax:** 01793 791487
Email: prebendal@aol.com

🛏 3 🛏 1 £50.00 🛏 1 £25.00 (£25.00)
V

The True Heart Inn — all year

Mr & Mrs B Hickton
The True Heart Inn, High Street,
Bishopstone, SWINDON SN6 8PH
☎ 01793 790080 **Fax:** 01793 790080

🛏 1 🛏 1 £40.00 (£25.00) **V**

ASHBURY

 SU2685 🥾 1km

☆ Ashdown House (Tel: 01488 72584)

The Village Stores — closed Xmas, New Year

Mrs J Schiff
The Village Stores, Ashbury,
SWINDON SN6 8NA
☎ 01793 710262

🛏 2 £40.00 (£25.00) **V**

The Village Stores
Ashbury, Swindon, Wiltshire

Tel: 01793 710262

Ashbury is a pretty village just half a mile
from The Ridgeway National Trail. Peter and
Jean-Anne Schiff own the Village Stores and
provide comfortable bed and breakfast
accommodation in their 18th century thatched
cottage. Guests are warmly welcomed and
will enjoy a traditional breakfast based on
local produce.

Rose and Crown Hotel — *all year*

Ms J A Blake
Rose and Crown Hotel, High Street,
Ashbury, SWINDON SN6 8NA
☎ 01793 710222 **Fax:** 01793 710029

🛏 5 🚲 4 £55.00 🛏 1 £40.00 (£40.00)
V 🏕 🚭 👫 🚫 ♿ **DRY** 🚲 🐾

WOOLSTONE

 SU2987 🥾 2km 📞

  ✕

Hickory House — *closed Xmas*

Mrs C Grist
Hickory House, Woolstone,
FARINGDON SN7 7QL
☎ 01367 820303 **Fax:** 01367 820958
Email: rlg@hickoryhouse.freeserve.co.uk

🚲 2 £42.00 (£25.00)   **DRY**
🚲 🚗

Tel:
**01367
820303**

Fax:
**01367
820958**

Hickory House

Hickory House, Woolstone, Oxfordshire

Comfortable en-suite bedrooms in self-contained extension in beautiful village.
Pub serving food is within two minutes walk from the house.

THE WHITE HORSE

Woolstone, Oxfordshire

Tel: **01367 820726**   *Fax:* **01367 820566**

16th Century inn situated under 'Uffington White Horse' in lovely olde world village of Woolstone.

All rooms en-suite with Sky TV. Hospitality trays, hairdryers etc.

In winter enjoy our log fires and in summer our lovely garden. We pride ourselves on serving freshly cooked local produce. A la carte reutaurant and bar meals.

The White Horse   *all year*

Mrs M Batty
The White Horse, Woolstone,
FARINGDON SN7 7QL
☎ 01367 820726 **Fax:** 01367 820566

🛏 4 🛏 2 🛏 1 £65.00 (£50.00) **V**

⚠ 🚫 📷 ⛩ ♿ **DRY** 🚲 🚗 👣
◆◆◆◆

UFFINGTON

SU3089 🏠 3km 📞

🫖 village hall Jun-Sep

⭐ Tom Brown's School Museum
(Tel: 01367 820259)

Britchcombe Countryside — *all year*

Mrs M Seymour
Britchcombe Countryside, Britchcombe
Farm, Uffington, FARINGDON SN7 7QJ
📞 01367 820667 **Mob:** 07940 325557

🏕 20 £3.00 🚐 10 £3.00 🎱 🔥 ♿

🔥 🚫 📷 🚻 ♿ **DRY** 🚲 🐾

🏠 Self-catering in mobile home on farm
3 bedrooms from £40/night, £90/week

Norton House — *closed Xmas*

Mrs F Oberman
Norton House, Broad Street, Uffington,
FARINGDON SN7 7RA
📞 01367 820230 **Fax:** 01367 820230
Email: 106436.145@compuserve.com

🛏 1 🛏 1 🛏 1 £38.00
🛏 1 £22.00 (£26.00) **V** 🔥 🚫 📷 🚻
🚫 **DRY** 🚲 🚗 🐾

Sower Hill Farm — *all year*

Mrs S Cox
Sower Hill Farm, Uffington,
FARINGDON SN7 7QH
📞 01367 820758

🛏 1 🛏 1 £40.00 🛏 1 £20.00
(£30.00) **V** 🔥 🚫 🚫 **DRY** 🚲 🐾

💲 3 £5.00 🅖 7 £1.00

FARINGDON

SU2895 🏠 9.5km
Town with range of services ℹ️

Sudbury House Hotel — *all year*

Mr A Ibbotson
Sudbury House Hotel, Folly Hill,
FARINGDON SN7 8AA
📞 01367 241272 **Fax:** 01367 242346
Email: sudburyhouse@cix.co.uk
Website: www.sudburyhouse.co.uk

🛏 39 🛏 10 🛏 4 £65.00 (£55.00)
V 🔥 🚫 📷 🚻 ♿ **DRY** 🚲 🐾
★★★

Section 2

Uffington Castle to Streatley

This 33 km stretch of The Ridgeway keeps to the high scarp edge of the open downland in Oxfordshire and Berkshire and includes the widest parts of the Trail and some of the best conditions underfoot. There's also lots of history to explore.

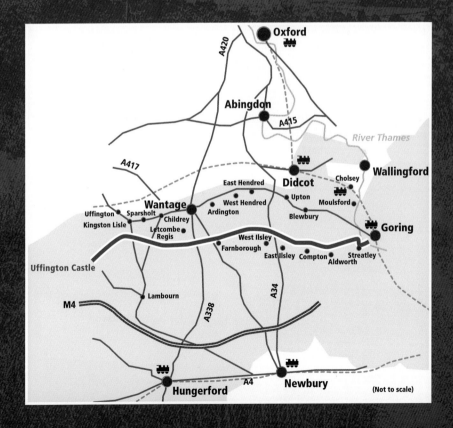

Oxford

A420

Abingdon

A415

River Thames

A417

Wallingford

East Hendred

Didcot

Cholsey

West Hendred

Upton

Moulsford

Wantage

Ardington

Uffington Sparsholt

Childrey

Blewbury

Kingston Lisle

Letcombe

Regis

Goring

West Ilsley

Farnborough

East Ilsley Compton Streatley

Uffington Castle

Aldworth

M4

Lambourn

A338

A34

Hungerford

A4 Newbury

(Not to scale)

A Taster

Rolling open downland to the south, punctuated in places by small woodlands, and fine views north into the Vale of White Horse and the Thames Valley are typical of this section. On a clear day you can see the hills in the distance behind which nestles Oxford and, further east, the Chiltern Hills through which The Ridgeway later travels. Dominating the view from many places are the cooling towers of Didcot power station just 10 km north, sometimes menacing and inappropriate but at other times strangely beautiful.

This is horse racing country and an early riser will encounter strings of racehorses exercising on the numerous gallops, long ribbons of well managed grass tracks, adjacent to The Ridgeway. The turf of the downland drains easily through the chalk just below creating excellent going for horses.

Small villages are strung out below to the north at the spring line where water seeps between different geological layers. Many of these are worth a visit to enjoy the local vernacular architecture which includes cottages built from chalk blocks quarried from the downs.

This section also negotiates the A34 north-south trunk road by an underpass. The noise of the traffic is counteracted to some extent by the colourful mural depicting local historical scenes painted by local people on the walls of the underpass.

Folly Clumb in the distance, south of Childrey

History

This section is steeped in history from prehistoric times right through to this century. The earliest monuments are the round barrows, burial chambers dating from Bronze Age times, roughly from 2000 to 750 BC. There are several close to The Ridgeway, including one in the area of woodland at Scutchamer's Knob above East Hendred which was excavated and ruthlessly dug away in 1842. Another lies within the width of the path a kilometre west of the B4494 road.

Two Iron Age forts grace this part of The Ridgeway, Uffington Castle and Segsbury Camp. Just a short distance from the former lies the most famous hill figure in the country, the Uffington White Horse, and below this Dragon Hill, a natural mound where, reputedly, St George killed his dragon. The bare chalk patch on the top is said to be where the blood of the dragon was spilt and no grass will now grow.

The Saxons have left their mark in this area with Wantage being the birth place of King Alfred who subsequently fought battles on the downs. Wantage also gave its name to Lord Wantage whose wife erected the monument to her husband on The Ridgeway just east of the B4494. His descendants still own the model farm and villages he built at the end of the last century.

A little further east of here and to the south lies the village of East Ilsley famous for its sheep fairs which only finished in the 1930s.

Statue of King Alfred
in Wantage Market Place

Maps

Landranger maps	174	Newbury and Wantage
Explorer maps	170	Abingdon, Wantage and Vale of White Horse
Pathfinder maps	1154 (SU28/38)	Lambourn Downs
	1155 (SU48/58)	Wantage (East) and Didcot (South)

Public Transport Information

National Rail all sections	24 hours a day 0345 484950 www.railtrack.co.uk
Oxfordshire County Council	01865 810405
West Berkshire Council	0118 9015900

Car Parking

The following are places close to or on The Ridgeway, other than villages or towns, with parking for vehicles - at some only for a few. Unfortunately theft from vehicles parked in the countryside does occasionally occur so please leave valuables at home.

Place	Map Grid Reference
National Trust car park for Uffington White Horse, south off B4507	SU 293866
On Ridgeway at Sparsholt Firs on the south side of the B4001, 4km south of Childrey.	SU 344851
On Ridgeway on the east side of B4494, 5km south of Wantage	SU 417843
On Ridgeway at Scutchamer's Knob, 3km south of E Hendred off the A417 east of wantage	SU 458851
On Ridgeway at Bury Down on minor road from A34 to W Ilsley (signed Ridgeway from A34)	SU 479841
On Ridgeway at end of Rectory Road, Streatley west off A417.	SU 567813

Taxis

Place	Name	Telephone Number
East Challow	Laser Cars	01235 762647/0973 627051
	Stuart's Taxis	01235 770608
Wantage	Gemini Cars	01235 764444/0800 0282219
Grove (near Wantage)	Grove Cabs	01235 772200
	Sapphire Cabs	01235 771212/772424
	Evenload Taxis	01235 762035
Chilton	A Rural Travel Service	01235 834469
Compton	Compton Passenger Service	01635 579076
Blewbury	Rural Connections	01235 851010
Didcot	Bob's	01235 512121
	Harold's	01235 812345
	Pryor's	01235 812345
Goring	Murdock's Taxi Service	01491 872029
	Goring Taxis	01491 873963
	M & J Taxis	01491 873253

Blewbury Down north of Compton

Water Taps

- with troughs for animals

Place	Map Grid Reference
Hill Barn Sparsholt	SU 338854
The Ridgeway Youth Hostel, Letcombe Regis	SU 393849
Ridgeway Down, Lockinge	SU 430846
Compton Down	SU 506823

Toilets

The Ridgeway Youth Hostel, Letcombe Regis	SU 393849

Police

Oxfordshire and Berkshire	01865 846000

Hospitals

Place	Telephone Number	Name
Swindon	01793 536231	Princess Margaret Hospital, Okus Road, Swindon
Wantage	01235 403801	Wantage Community Hospital, Garston Lane, Wantage
Didcot	01235 517900	Didcot Hospital, Wantage Road, Didcot. (weekdays 6pm - 8am, weekends/bank holidays 24 hours)

Vets

Place	Name	Telephone Number
Lambourn	Ridgeway Group	01488 71999
Faringdon	Danetree	01367 242777
	Elms Surgery	01367 242416
Wantage	Abivale Group	01235 770333
	Danetree	01235 770227
West Ilsley	Clemenger	01635 281344
Didcot	Abivale Group	01235 511553
	Larkmead Group	01235 814991
Cholsey	Larkmead Group	01491 651479

Farriers

Place	Name	Telephone Number
Lambourn	Alderton	01488 72583
	Charles	01488 71310/0831 595073
	Pickford	01488 72613

Saddlers

Place	Name	Telephone Number
Lambourn	Wicks	01488 71766
Faringdon	S & J M Cooper	01367 240517
Goosey		
(near Faringdon)	Asti Stud Saddlery	01367 710288
Denchworth	Denchworth Equestrian	
(near Wantage)	Supplies	01235 868175
Blewbury	Arena Saddlery	01235 850725/0402 685072

Mountain Bike Hire

Place	Name	Telephone Number
Abingdon	Braggs	01235 520034
	Pedal power	01235 525123

Bike Repairs

Place	Name	Telephone Number
Wantage	Ridgeway Cycles	01235 764445
	GMC	01235 764204
Didcot	Dentons	01235 816566
Abingdon	Braggs	01235 520034
	Pedal power	01235 525123
	Behind Bars	01235 535624

Tourist Information Centres

★ offers accommodation booking service

Place	Address/Opening Hours
★ Faringdon	7a Market Place, Faringdon SN7 7HL Tel/Fax: 01367 242191 Opening hours: Summer (1 Apr-31 Oct) Mon-Fri 10:00-13:00, 13:30-17:00, Sat 10:00-13:00 Winter (1 Nov-31 Mar) Mon-Sat 10:00-13:00
★ Wantage	19 Church Street, Wantage OX12 8BL Tel/Fax: 01235 760167 Opening hours: All year: Tue-Sat 10:30-16:30, Sun 14:30-17.00
★ Abingdon	25 Bridge Street, Abingdon OX14 3HN Tel: 01235 522711 Fax: 01235 535245 Opening hours: Summer (1 Apr-31 Oct) Mon-Sat 10:00-17:00 Winter (1 Nov-31 Mar) Mon-Fri 10:00-16:00, Sat 09:30-14:30
★ Didcot	Station Road Car Park, Didcoty OX11 7NR Tel/Fax: 01235 813243 Opening hours: Summer (Jul-Aug) daily 10:00-17:00 Winter (Sep-Jun) Mon-Sat 10:00-16:00

Wantage Monument south of Ardington

KINGSTON LISLE

SU3287 △ 2km 📞

🍺 ▯▮▯▯▯▯▯▯ ✕ ▮▮▯▯▯▯▯▯
  S M T W T F S   S M T W T F S

Down Barn Farm

**Down Barn Farm, Sparsholt,
Wantage, Oxfordshire.**

Down Barn Farm stands in complete isolation and total peace and quiet in a hollow of the downs $1/4$ mile from The Ridgeway. It is a working farm producing organic beef and pork. Horses are trained for Endurance Riding.

Tel: **01367 820272**

Mobile: **0777 5678244**

SPARSHOLT

SU3487 △ 3km 📞

🍺 ▯▯▯▯▯▯▯▯ ✕ ▮▯▯▯▯▯▯▯
  S M T W T F S   S M T W T F S

| Down Barn Farm | closed Xmas | ⚔ ♞ |

Mrs P Reid
Down Barn Farm, Sparsholt Down,
WANTAGE OX12 9XD
☎ 01367 820272 **Mob:** 0777 5678 244

🛏 1 🛏 2 £40.00 (£25.00) **V** 🖊
🚫 except Sundays 🔌 ⛹ 🚫 ♿ **DRY**
🚲 🥾 ⛰ 600m south of Ridgeway

⛺ 2 £5.00 🚐 1 £10.00 🗐 🔧 🔧 🍷 ⊙

💲 3 £8.00 🌀 6 £5.00

| Westcot Lodge | all year |

Mrs P Upton
Westcot Lodge, Westcot, WANTAGE
OX12 9QA
☎ 01235 751251

🛏 1 🛏 1 £50.00

🛏 1 £30.00 (£50.00) **V** 🖊 🚫 ⛹ 🚫
DRY 🚲 🚗 🥾

55

The Star Inn *all year*

Mr & Mrs A J Fowles
The Star Inn, Watery Lane, Sparsholt,
WANTAGE OX12 9PL
☎ 01235 751001 **Fax:** 01235 751539

🛏 2 🛌 5 🛌 1 £55.00 (£55.00)

THE STAR INN

Watery Lane, Sparsholt, Oxfordshire

☎ **01235 751539/751001**

~ Beautiful village setting ~

FREE HOUSE

Separate non-smoking dining room -
lunches - evening meals - garden - car
parking -children welcome - real ales -
eight en-suite rooms in quiet annexe.

CHILDREY

SU3687 🥾 4km

Ridgeway House B&B *all year*

Mrs M A Roberts
Ridgeway House B&B, West Street,
Childrey, WANTAGE OX12 9UL
☎ 01235 751538 **Mob:** 0374 182154
Fax: 01235 751538 **Email:**
robertsfamily@compuserve.com

🛌 2 £45.00 (£29.00) **V**

LETCOMBE REGIS

SU3886 🥾 2km

Quince Cottage *all year*

Mrs L Boden
Quince Cottage, Letcombe Regis,
WANTAGE OX12 9JP
☎ 01235 763652

🛌 1 £40.00 (£25.00) **V**

The Old Vicarage — *all year*

Mrs J Barton
The Old Vicarage, Letcombe Regis,
WANTAGE OX12 9JP
☎ 01235 765827 **Fax:** 01235 765827

🛏 2 🛏 1 £45.00 🛏 1 £22.00 (£30.00)
V 🝙 🌑 🕇 🚫 **DRY** 🚲 🚗 🚶

Cottage in Letcombe Bassett

The Old Vicarage

Letcombe Regis, Wantage, Oxfordshire
Tel/Fax: **01235 765827**

A substantial Victorian vicarage set in a
delightful garden offering comfortable
accommodation. Warm welcome in a real
family home. Near the pub in a pretty
downland village just one mile from
The Ridgeway.

Gwastad — *all year*

J Williams
Gwastad
Bassett Road, Letcombe Regis
WANTAGE OX12 9JP
☎ 01235 766240

🛏 2 £40.00 (£20.00) 🝙 🌑 🕇 🚫
DRY 🚲

YHA Ridgeway Centre — *phone ahead*

YHA Ridgeway Centre, Court Hill,
Letcombe Regis, WANTAGE OX12 9NE
☎ 01235 760253 **Fax:** 01235 768865

V 🝙 🌑 🕇 🚫 ♿ **DRY** 🚲
🛏 Dormitory accommodation £9.40/head

🏕 20 £4.50   🚻 📷 🔲

🍲 4 £8.50

Lockinge Kiln Farm

The Ridgeway, Wantage, Oxfordshire ~ *Tel/Fax*: 01235 763308

Comfortable farmhouse enjoying a quiet country location,
just ¹/₂ mile south of The Ridgeway. Ideal walking – riding – cycling.

Grid Reference: SU 427834

WANTAGE

⊹ **SU4088** 🏘 **4km Market town with range of services** ℹ️

☆ Vale & Downland Museum
(Tel: 01235 771447)

Gwithian   *all year*

Mrs G Dawn Cox
Gwithian, 2 The Pound, Charlton,
WANTAGE OX12 7HN
☎ 01235 762561

🛏 1 🛏 1 £32.00 (£18.00) **V** 🧖
🚭 🚫 **DRY** 🚲 🚗

Lockinge Kiln Farm   *closed Xmas*

Mrs S Cowan
Lockinge Kiln Farm, The Ridgeway,
WANTAGE OX12 8PA
☎ 01235 763308 **Fax:** 01235 763308
Email: stellacowan@hotmail.com

🛏 1 🛏 2 £38.00 (£22.00) **V** 🧖
🚫 🔌 ♿ over 10 years 🚭 **DRY** 🚲
🧖 🍴 800m south of Ridgeway

🏅 2 £8.00 🏅 6 £4.00

The Bell Inn   *all year*

Mr & Mrs Williams
The Bell Inn, Market Place, WANTAGE
OX12 8AH
☎ 01235 763718

🛏 2 🛏 3 🛏 6 £40.00
🛏 6 £20.00 (£25.00) **V** 🧖 🚫 🔌 ♿

ARDINGTON

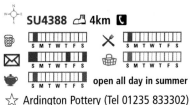

SU4388 🥾 4km 📞

☆ Ardington Pottery (Tel 01235 833302)

open all day in summer

Downland Equestrian *closed Xmas Day*

Mrs V Haigh
Downland Equestrian, Orpwood House,
Ardington, WANTAGE OX12 8PN
☎ 01235 833300 **Fax:** 01235 820950

🛏 3 🛏 1 £48.00 🛏 3 £26.00 (£26.00)
V 🔥 🚫 🚻 🚭 DRY 🚲 🚗 🦮

⒮ 8 £14.00 Ⓖ 8 £8.00

WEST HENDRED

SU4488 🥾 4km 📞

EAST HENDRED

SU4688 🥾 4km 📞

☆ Champs Chapel Museum
(Tel: 01235 833312/833471)

Monks Court *all year*

Mrs S Turnbull
Monks Court, Newbury Road, East
Hendred, WANTAGE OX12 8LG
☎ 01235 833797 **Fax:** 01235 862554
Email: susie@monkscourt.demon.co.uk

🛏 1 £40.00 🛏 1 £20.00 (£25.00) V
🚫 🖼 🚻 🚭 ♿ DRY 🚲 🚗 🦮

⒮ 1 £5.00 Ⓖ 2 £5.00

Ridgeway Lodge Hotel *all year*

Mrs A Newman
Ridgeway Lodge Hotel, Skeats Bush,
East Hendred, WANTAGE OX12 8LH
☎ 01235 833360 **Fax:** 01235 820389

🛏 3 🛏 2 🛏 2 £60.00
🛏 4 £38.00 (£38.00)

V 🔥 🚫 🖼 🚻 ♿ DRY 🚲 🚗

WEST ILSLEY

SU4782 ⚲ 2km ☎

🍺 S M T W T F S   ✕ S M T W T F S
✉ S M T W T F S   🧺 S M T W T F S

CHILTON

SU4986 ⚲ 2km ☎

🍺 S M T W T F S   ✕ S M T W T F S
✉ S M T W T F S   🧺 S M T W T F S
🫖 S M T W T F S

EAST ILSLEY

SU4981 ⚲ 2km ☎

🍺 S M T W T F S   ✕ S M T W T F S

UPTON

SU5186 ⚲ 4km ☎

🍺 S M T W T F S   ✕ S M T W T F S
✉ S M T W T F S

COMPTON

SU5280 ⚲ 2km ☎

🍺 S M T W T F S   ✕ S M T W T F S
✉ S M T W T F S   🧺 S M T W T F S

£ Midland

Memorial window to John Betjeman by John
Piper in Farnborough church

Compton Swan Hotel   *all year*

Mr G Mitchell
Compton Swan Hotel, High Street,
Compton, NEWBURY RG20 6NJ
☎ 01635 578269 **Fax:** 01635 578765
Email: garry@comptonswan.freeserve.co.uk
Web: www.smoothhound.co.uk/hotels
/comptons

🛏 2 🛏 2 🛏 1 £55.00
🛏 1 £44.00 (£44.00)
V 🅰 🚫 🈁 🕴 🚭 ♿ DRY 🚲
🚗 🗺

BLEWBURY

SU5385 ⛰ 4km 📞 ⓘ

Blewbury Inn *closed Xmas Day*

Mr F Peigné
Blewbury Inn, London Road, Blewbury,
DIDCOT OX11 9PD
☎ 01235 850496

🛏 1 🛌 1 £50.00 (£40.00)

V 🕭 🚫 🐕 ♀♂ 🚫 🚵

ALDWORTH

SU5579 ⛰ 2km 📞

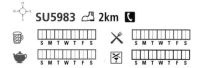

MOULSFORD

SU5983 ⛰ 2km 📞

🍺 ▥ ✕ ▥
🫖 ▥ 🍴 ▥

White House *closed Xmas, New Year*

Mrs M Watsham
White House, Moulsford, WALLINGFORD
OX10 9JD
☎ 01491 651397 **Mob:** 0831 372243
Fax: 01491 652560

🛏 1 🛌 1 £45.00
🛌 1 £25.00 (£30.00)

V 🕭 🚫 ♀♂ 🚫 **DRY** 🚲 🚶

◆◆◆◆◆

CHOLSEY

SU5886 ⛰ 6km 📞

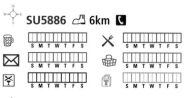

☆ **Cholsey & Wallingford Railway**
(Tel: 01491 835067)

The Well Cottage *all year*

Mrs J Alexander
The Well Cottage, Caps Lane, Cholsey,
WALLINGFORD OX10 9HQ
☎ 01491 651959 **Mob:** 07887 958920

🛌 2 £40.00 (£20.00)

V 🐕 ♀♂ ♿ **DRY** 🚲 🚶

STREATLEY

SU5980 on The Ridgeway

S M T W T F S   ✕   S M T W T F S

☆ Beale Park (Tel: 0118 984 5172);
Basildon Park (Tel: 0118 984 3040)

YHA Streatley   *phone ahead*

YHA Streatley, Hill House, Reading Road,
Streatley, READING RG8 9JJ
☎ 01491 872278 **Fax:** 01491 873056
Email: streatley@yha.org.uk

V 🏕 ⊘ ⁂ ⊘ DRY 🚲 ⚑
Dormitory accommodation £10.85/adult

YOUTH HOSTELS
Court Hill, Streatley, Bradenham and Ivinghoe

There are four Youth Hostels - at Court Hill, Streatley,
Bradenham and Ivinghoe - along The Ridgeway National
Trail, all offering affordable, friendly and comfortable
accommodation in family rooms or dormitories. Prices
start from £7.25 per night and meals are excellent value
at £4.80 for evening and £3.30 for full breakfast. The
YHA is a membership organisation; non-members are
welcome to join on arrival at any Youth Hostel.

• *Court Hill*
• *Streatley*
• *Bradenham*
• *Ivinghoe*

Section 3

Streatley to Chinnor

This 33 km section of The Ridgeway in Oxfordshire is full of variety and charm. It passes through a couple of villages as it follows the River Thames before heading into the more wooded, yet still undulating, Chiltern Hills via an ancient Grim's Ditch and finishes on the wide track of the old Icknield Way.

A Taster

Water, woodlands and small villages are features of this part of The Ridgeway, contrasting considerably with the open and more remote countryside of Sections One and Two.

England's most famous river, the River Thames, is your companion for the first few kilometres and as you follow it you'll pass through water meadows grazed by cattle and the two lovely villages of South and North Stoke. On the opposite bank, another National Trail runs, The Thames Path which The Ridgeway crossed at Goring bridge. Then as you strike east you'll walk on a narrow secluded path alongside a Grim's Ditch for a considerable distance, much of it surrounded by woodland bright with bluebells and wood anemones during spring.

From the village of Nuffield you turn north and soon reach the small hamlet of Swyncombe, an area which is probably one of the remotest and loveliest parts of the Chilterns. Here, the small flint church of St Botolph's has been beautifully restored.

Descending from Swyncombe to near the base of the scarp, The Ridgeway picks up the Upper Icknield Way and follows this broad track for the remaining 13 kilometres to Chinnor. This latter part can be enjoyed by horseriders and cyclists as well as walkers and during wet times of the year gets muddy in places. The first 8 km of this Icknield Way section can also legally be used by drivers of vehicles.

Agriculture along this section is varied and includes a variety of crops and animal grazing. Many of the woodlands in the area, too, are managed for timber.

A few kilometres before Chinnor you'll cross the M40 by an underpass where the motorway slices through the Aston Rowant Nature Reserve in a deep cutting.

South Stoke church

64

History

The variety of landscape in this section is also reflected in the history of the area with the National Trail encountering amongst other things four important trading routes; the prehistoric Icknield Way, the River Thames used continuously for trading, the Great Western Railway constructed in the 19th century and, of course, today's motorway. The railway makes its impact unpleasantly felt as you initially walk north from Goring, but further along the Thames your path passes beneath Brunel's splendid bridge built in 1839 with its skewed arches and unusual brickwork - well worth a look.

Grim's Ditch is a fascinating ancient earthwork which accompanies you for several kilometres. It's amazing to think such a ditch was constructed using just antler picks as tools. Before you reach the Icknield Way you walk through several areas of woodland dominated by beech trees, and views of others stay with you to Chinnor.

Most of the beech trees you see today have been planted. From the 17th century the wood has been used, initially to supply a cheap source of fuel and charcoal for London and then in the last century by craftsmen. Tent-peg makers and chair leg turners, the bodgers, flourished throughout the Chilterns with the industry centred on High Wycombe. Few bodgers remain but the woodlands still have a commercial and leisure value.

As you pass Watlington it's worth looking to the south to the hillside rearing above you to spy the Watlington White Mark, another of the chalk figures cut into the hills through which The Ridgeway wanders.

Maps		
Landranger maps	174	Newbury and Wantage
	175	Reading and Windsor
	165	Aylesbury and leighton Buzzard
Explorer maps	171	Chiltern Hills West
Pathfinder maps	1155 (SU48/58)	Wantage (East) and Didcot (South)
	1156 (SU68/78)	Henley-on-Thames and Wallingford
	1137 (SU69/79)	Watlington and Stokenchurch
	1117 (SP60/70)	Thame

Public Transport Information

National Rail all sections   24 hours a day 0345 484950
www.railtrack.co.uk
Oxfordshire County Council   01865 810405

Car Parking

The following are places close to or on The Ridgeway, other than villages or towns, with parking for vehicles - at some only for a few. Unfortunately theft from vehicles parked in the countryside does occasionally occur so please leave valuables at home.

Place	Map Grid Reference
Goring on Thames public car park	SU 599807
On Ridgeway on west side of minor road, 1.5 km from Britwell Salome heading southeast	SU 681922
On Ridgeway on east side of Hill Road, minor road to Christmas Common 1 km southeast of Watlington	SU 698940
On Ridgeway on east side of minor road to Bledlow Ridge 1 km south of Chinnor	SP 761003

Grim's Ditch east of Wallingford

Taxis

Place	Name	Telephone Number
Goring	Murdock's Taxi Service	01491 872029
	Goring Taxis	01491 873963
	M & S Taxis	01491 873253
Wallingford	Hills	01491 837022/837497
Benson	A Cabs	01491 839982
	Pontings Taxis	01491 826679
Ewelme	Bushers Taxis	01491 826161/0385 296392
Henley-on-Thames	Chiltern Taxis	01491 578899
	County Cars	01491 579696
	Harris Taxis	01491 577036
Thame	English Chauffeur Drive	01844 260555/215483
	Bambrook Garage	01844 212885
	Thame Taxis	01844 216161/214433/215000
Chinnor	Chinnor Cabs	01844 353637
Bledlow Ridge	Ridge Rentals	01494 481568

Water Taps

- with troughs for animals

Place	Map Grid Reference
Grimsdyke Cottage, Grim's Ditch	SU 660872
Church, Nuffield (on the wall)	SU 667874

- White Mark Farm Camp Site, Watlington
  (March-October) SU 697939

Toilets

Place	Map Grid Reference
Goring-on-Thames (Car Park off Station Road)	SU 660872
White Mark Farm Camp Site, Watlington (March-October)	SU 697939
Watlington (High Street)	SU 689945

Police

Oxfordshire   01865 846000

Hospitals

Place	Telephone Number	Address
Wallingford	01491 835533	Wallingford Community Hospital, Reading Road, Wallingford.

Vets

Place	Name	Telephone Number
Wallingford	Dovecourt Group	01491 839043
Watlington	Crossroads	01491 612799
Thame/Chinnor	Sprinz and Nash	01844 212000

Farriers

Place	Name	Telephone Number
Watlington	Smith	01491 612872
Chalgrove	Selwyn Mobile Farrier	0378 601831

Saddlers

Place	Name	Telephone Number
Stokenchurch	Equitana Equestrian	01494 484106

Mountain Bike Hire

Place	Name	Telephone Number
Wallingford	Rides on Air	01491 836289

Bike Repairs

Place	Name	Telephone Number
Pangbourne	Mountain High	0118 984 1851
Wallingford	Rides on Air	01491 836289
Thame	Thame Cycles	01844 261520

Tourist Information Centres

★ offers accommodation booking service

Place	Address/Opening Hours
★ Wallingford	Town Hall, Market Place, Wallingford OX10 0EG Tel: 01491 826972 Fax: 01491 832925 Opening hours: All year: Mon-Sat 09:30-17:00
★ Thame (★ Visitors to office only)	Market House, North Street, Thame OX9 3HH Tel/fax: 01844 212834 Opening hours: August: Mon-Fri 09:30-17:00, Sat 10:00-16:00, Sun/Bank Hols 10:00-15:00 Rest of year: Mon-Fri 09:30-17:00, Sat 10:00-16:0

GORING

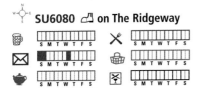

SU6080 on The Ridgeway

£ Lloyds; HSBC

Miller of Mansfield — all year

Mr M Williamson
Miller of Mansfield, High Street, Goring-on-Thames, READING RG8 9AW
☎ 01491 872829 **Fax:** 01491 874200

2 2 1 £65.50
4 £49.50 (£49.50)

V ♦♦♦

14 Mountfield — all year

Mrs N Ewen
14 Mountfield, Wallingford Road, Goring-on-Thames, READING RG8 0BE
☎ 01491 872029 **Fax:** 01491 872029

1 £45.00 1 £25.00 (£25.00)

V ♦♦

Northview House — all year

Mrs I Sheppard
Northview House, Farm Road, Goring-on-Thames, READING RG8 0AA
☎ 01491 872184 **Mob:** 0385 761851
Email: HI@goring-on-thames.freeserve.co.uk

2 1 £35.00 (£17.50)

Caring for the Chilterns

You can help the Chilterns by

• Enjoying, understanding and caring for the chilterns

• Leaving your car at home

• Showing respect to other users of the countryside

• Supporting the local economy - buy local products and services

• Not disrupting the activities of those who make their living from the countryside

• Taking pride in the Chilterns - follow the Country Code

The Chilterns
Area of Outstanding Natural Beauty

Looking from Ladies Walk to Jacob's Tent, Swyncombe

Queens Arms   *all year*

Mr M Perrett
Queens Arms, Reading Road, Goring-on-Thames, READING RG8 0ER
☎ 01491 872825

🛏 1 🛏 1 £45.00
🛏 1 £25.00 (£25.00) ♿ 🚭

The Catherine Wheel   *all year*

Mrs D M Kerr
The Catherine Wheel, Station Road, Goring-on-Thames, READING RG8 9HB
☎ 01491 872379

🛏 2 🛏 1 £40.00 (£25.00)

V

 whole house from £380/week, sleeps 6

The John Barleycorn   *all year*

Mr A Fincham
The John Barleycorn, Manor Road, Goring-on-Thames, READING RG8 9DP
☎ 01491 872509

🛏 2 🛏 1 🛏 1 £40.00
🛏 2 £25.00 (£30.00)

V ♦

SOUTH STOKE

 SU6083 on The Ridgeway

NORTH STOKE

 SU6186 on The Ridgeway

Footpath Cottage   *all year*

Mrs R G Tanner
Footpath Cottage, The Street, North Stoke, WALLINGFORD OX10 6BJ
☎ 01491 839763

🛏 2 £38.00 🛏 1 £20.00 (£25.00)

V

Brunel's bridge north of South Stoke

CROWMARSH GIFFORD

⌖ SU6189 ⌂ 1km 📞

🍺 |||||||||||| S M T W T F S ✕ |||||||||||| S M T W T F S

✉ |||||||||||| S M T W T F S 🧺 |||||||||||| S M T W T F S

Little Gables   *all year*

Mrs J Reeves
Little Gables, 166 Crowmarsh Hill,
WALLINGFORD OX10 8BG
☎ 01491 837834 **Fax:** 01491 837834
Email: jfreeves@globalnet.co.uk

🛏 2 🛏 2 🛏 2 £50.00
🛏 1 £30.00 (£35.00)

V 🎒 ⓝ 🍴 🚭 DRY 🚲 🚶
◆◆◆◆

Blenheim Farm House   *closed Xmas*

Mrs J Sarreti
Blenheim Farm House, Icknield Way,
WALLINGFORD OX10 6PR
☎ 01491 832368 **Fax:** 01491 832273
Email: peter.sarreti@which.net

🛏 1 £40.00 🛏 1 £20.00 (£35.00)

V ⓝ 🚭 DRY 🚲 🚶 ⚑ 200m
north of Ridgeway near Oakley Wood

Bridge Villa Caravan/Camp Site *closed Jan* ⛺

Mr E L Townsend
Bridge Villa Caravan & Camp Site,
The Street, Crowmarsh Gifford,
WALLINGFORD OX10 8HB
☎ 01491 836860 **Mob:** 0410 452429
Fax: 01491 839103 **Website:**
www.oxfordonline.co.uk/bridgevilla

⛺ 50 £4.00 🚐 50 £6.00

ⓝ 🔌 🚲 🖥 🔥 🔥 ♿ 🛒

Riverside Park/Caravan Site *closed Oct-Mar* ⛺

Mr G Kearney
Riverside Park & Caravan Site, The Street,
Wallingford Bridge, Crowmarsh Gifford,
WALLINGFORD OX10 8EB
☎ 01491 835232 or 01865 341035
Fax: 01491 835232 or 01865 341035

⛺ 28 £5.90 🚐 28 £5.90

ⓝ ♿ 🖥 🔥 🔥 ♿ 🛒

Goring Lock

WALLINGFORD

⌖ **SU6089** 👢 **2km Market town with range of services** ℹ️

☆ Wallingford Museum (Tel: 01491 835065)

'Home from Home'   *closed 21 Dec - 4 Jan*

Mrs C Scott
'Home from Home', 1A St Mary's Street,
WALLINGFORD OX10 0EL
☎ 01491 834706

🛏 1 🛏 1 £35.00 (£25.00)

V 🏞 🅾 👫 🚫 **DRY** 🚲 🚗 👟

---

52 Blackstone Road   *closed Xmas*

Mrs E J Barnard
52 Blackstone Road,
WALLINGFORD OX10 8JL
☎ 01491 839339

🛏 1 £30.00 🛏 1 £15.00 (£18.00)

🅾 🚫 **DRY** 🚲 👟

The George Hotel   *all year*

Mr O Round-Turner
The George Hotel, High Street,
WALLINGFORD OX10 0BS
☎ 01491 836665 **Fax:** 01491 825359

🛏 11 🛏 14 🛏 1 £78.00
🛏 13 £48.00 (£68.00)

V 🏞 🅾 👫 **DRY** 🚲 👟 ★★★

The Studio   *all year*

Mrs P Smith
The Studio, 85 Wantage Road,
WALLINGFORD OX10 0LT
☎ 01491 837277 **Fax:** 01491 825036

🛏 1 🛏 1 £40.00
🛏 2 £20.00 (£35.00)

🅾 🖼 👫 🚫 **DRY** 🚲 👟

BENSON

⌖ **SU6191** 👢 **2km** 📞 ⓘ

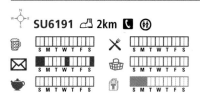

£ Midland cashpoint at BP garage 🖃
☆ Veteran Cycle Museum
(Tel: 01491 838414)

73

Fyfield Manor — *closed Xmas*

Mrs C Brown
Fyfield Manor, Brook Street, Benson,
WALLINGFORD OX10 6HA
☎ 01491 835184 **Fax:** 01491 825635

🛏 1 🛏 1 £50.00 (£30.00)

V 🚵 ⊘ ♟ over 10 yrs ⊗ **DRY** 🚲

Hale Farm — *closed Oct - Easter*

Mrs A H Belcher
Hale Farm, Benson,
WALLINGFORD OX10 6NE
☎ 01491 836818

🛏 1 🛏 1 £32.00 🛏 1 £16.00
(£16.00)

V 🚵 ⊘ ♟ ⊗ **DRY** 🚲 🚗
Paddock accommodation for horses by
prior arrangement

NUFFIELD

SU6787 on The Ridgeway

S M T W T F S   ✕ S M T W T F S

☎ ☆ **Nuffield Place (Tel: 01491
641224)**

Mays Farm — *all year*

Mrs P Passmore
Mays Farm, Nuffield, Ewelme,
WALLINGFORD OX10 6QF
☎ 01491 641294 **Fax:** 01491 641697
Email: Mays.Farm@tesco.net

🛏 1 🛏 1 £40.00
🛏 1 £25.00 (£28.00)

V 🚵 ⊘ ♟ ⊗ **DRY** 🚗 ◆◆◆◆

The Rectory — *all year*

Mr J Shearer
The Rectory, Nuffield,
HENLEY-ON-THAMES RG9 5SN
☎ 01491 641305 **Fax:** 01491 641305

🛏 1 🛏 1 🛏 1 £36.00
🛏 1 £20.00 (£20.00) V 🚵 ⊘ ♟
⊗ ♿ **DRY** 🚲

⛺ 5 £2.00 🚐 1 £5.00

2 £5.00

PARK CORNER

 SU6988 ⌂ 2km

 **Parkcorner Farm House** *all year*

Mrs S M Rutter
Parkcorner Farm House, Park Corner,
Nettlebed, HENLEY-ON-THAMES RG9 6DX
☎ 01491 641450

🛏 2 £45.00 🛏 1 £25.00 (£25.00)

⊗ 🏠 🚶 ⊘ DRY 🐾

ⓢ 2 £8.00

PISHILL

 SU7289 ⌂ 5km
🍺 [SMTWTFS] ✕ [SMTWTFS]

Bank Farm *all year*

Mrs E Lakey
Bank Farm, Pishill, HENLEY-ON-THAMES
RG9 6HJ
☎ 01491 638601 **Fax:** 01491 638601
Email: bankfarm@compuserve.com

🛏 1 £40.00 🛏 1 £15.00 (£20.00)

V 🏕 ⊗ 🏠 🚶 ⊘ DRY 🚲 🚗
◆◆

ⓖ 5 £3.00

Orchard House *all year*

Mrs J Connolly
Orchard House, Pishill, HENLEY-ON-
THAMES RG9 6HJ
☎ 01491 638351 **Fax:** 01491 638351

🛏 2 🛏 1 🛏 1 £45.00 (£25.00)

V 🏕 ⊗ 🏠 🚶 ⊘ DRY 🚲 🚗 🐾
🛄 luggage transport at weekends only

WATLINGTON

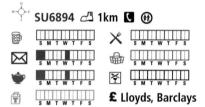 SU6894 ⌂ 1km 🔋 Ⓗ

🍺 [SMTWTFS] ✕ [SMTWTFS]
✉ [SMTWTFS] 🛒 [SMTWTFS]
🫖 [SMTWTFS] 🎫 [SMTWTFS]
🗑 [SMTWTFS] **£ Lloyds, Barclays**

West Meadow *all year*

Mrs L Fear
West Meadow, 28 The Goggs,
WATLINGTON OX9 5JX
☎ 01491 613278 **Fax:** 01491 612762

🛏 1 £40.00 (£28.00)

V 🏕 ⊗ 🚶 ⊘ DRY 🚲

 **White Mark Farm** *closed Nov - Feb*

Mr & Mrs J Williams
White Mark Farm, 82 Hill Road,
WATLINGTON OX9 5AF
☎ 01491 612295

🔥 many £3.00-£5.00

🚫 ▣ 🚲 🛏 🧺 🚰 👫

Woodgate Orchard Cottage *all year*

R Roberts
Woodgate Orchard Cottage, Howe Road,
WATLINGTON OX9 5EL
☎ 01491 612675 **Fax:** 01491 612675
Email: mailbox@wochr.freeserve.co.uk

🛏 2 🛌 1 £48.00 (£28.00)

V 🔥 🚫 👫 🚫 **DRY** 🚲 🚗 👣
🔋 organic food

CHALGROVE

 ⊕ SU6397 👢 7km ☎

CORNERSTONES

Cornerstones *closed Xmas, New Year*

Mrs M Duxbury
Cornerstones, 1 Cromwell Close,
Chalgrove, OXFORD OX44 7SE
☎ 01865 890298 **Mob:** 0780 8658013

🛌 2 £35.00 (£23.00)

V 🔥 🚫 except Sundays ▣ 👫 🚫 ♿
DRY 🚲 🚗 👣 ◆◆◆

LEWKNOR

 ⊕ SU7197 👢 1km ☎

☆ Cowleaze Wood Sculpture Trail

POSTCOMBE

 ⊕ SU7099 👢 2.5km ☎

Beech Farm *all year*

Mrs J Graham
Beech Farm, Salt Lane, Postcombe,
THAME OX9 7EE
☎ 01844 281240 **Mob:** 0973 506443

🛏 1 🛌 1 £45.00 (£30.00) V 🔥
🚫 ▣ 👫 🚫 ♿ **DRY** 🚲 🚗 👣

Spindle

ASTON ROWANT

SU7298 🥾 1km 📞

🍺 |S M T W T F S| ✕ |S M T W T F S|

Peel Guest House — all year

Mrs E Hunt
Peel Guest House, London Road, Aston
Rowant, WATLINGTON OX9 5SA
☎ 01844 351310

£50
£20 dep.
A4D

🛏 2 £42.00 🛏 1 £21.00 (£32.00)

V 🌶 🗺 🎏 ‍👫 ♿ 🚲

SYDENHAM

SP7301 🥾 4km 📞

🍺 |S M T W T F S| ✕ |S M T W T F S|

Inn at Emmington — all year

Mr P Matthews
Inn at Emmington, Thame Road,
Sydenham, CHINNOR OX9 4LD
☎ 01844 351367 **Fax:** 01844 351967
Email: emmington@hotmail.com
Website: www.innatemmington.co.uk

🛏 3 🛏 2 🛏 1 £55.00
🛏 3 £48.00 (£48.00)

V 🌶 🌶 🗺 ‍👫 ♿ DRY 🚲 🚗

CHINNOR

SP7500 🥾 1km 📞 ⚠

🍺 |S M T W T F S| ✕ |S M T W T F S|
✉ |S M T W T F S| 🧺 |S M T W T F S|
🍵 |S M T W T F S| 🎁 |S M T W T F S|
🥫 |S M T W T F S|

☆ Chinnor & Princes Risborough Steam
Railway (Tel: 01844 353535)

BLEDLOW

SP7702 🥾 1km 📞

🍺 |S M T W T F S| ✕ |S M T W T F S|

Cross Lanes Guest House — all year

Mr R Coulter
Cross Lanes Guest House, Bledlow,
PRINCES RISBOROUGH HP27 9PF
☎ 01844 345339 **Fax:** 01844 274165

🛏 2 🛏 1 £54.00 (£44.00)

V 🌶 🌶 🚭 ♿ DRY 🚲 🚗
◆◆◆◆

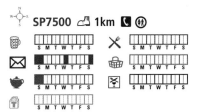

From Coombe Hill

Section 4

Chinnor to Ivinghoe Beacon

This 37 km eastern stretch of The Ridgeway wanders its way through wonderful wooded parts of the Chiltern Hills before emerging, just a few kilometres from its finish, into more open downland countryside reminiscent of the landscape surrounding its earlier stages. Keeping mainly to quiet footpaths, the Trail skirts around or dips into a few Chiltern settlements where welcome refreshments are easily available.

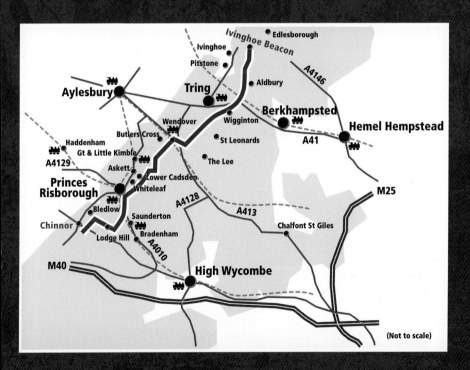

(Not to scale)

A Taster

Dominated by fine beech woodlands for which the Chiltern Hills are justly famous, this countryside however offers more than just trees. Probably the most undulating with several usually reasonably gentle climbs in and out of valleys, this section of The Ridgeway gives some marvellous experiences.

One minute you may be walking up a sheltered slope amongst the tall, straight, grey trunks of beeches and the next you'll have emerged into some fine unimproved chalk grassland boasting a great variety of wild flowers and insects with tremendous views across the Vale of Aylesbury. Or, turning a corner you'll reach the edge of a wood and have a view, framed by branches, of a secluded valley with just a small brick and timber farm complex nestling below you.

Agriculture is varied with crops grown in places, and sheep, cattle and horses grazed elsewhere. Many places are in fact nature reserves where the sheep and cattle are essential elements of the management to ensure the traditional chalk grasslands remain free of scrub and rich in wild species. The woodlands, too, are not just places for leisure as many are managed commercially for their timber.

You pass close to Princes Risborough and through the centre of Wendover, both typical and attractive small Chilterns towns, as well as going near some lovely villages. On Coombe Hill, marked by its monument, you will find yourself at the highest point of the Chiltern Hills with views on a clear day, extending as far as the Berkshire Downs and the Cotswolds. Just beyond Tring you reach the busy A41 trunk road but you cross it high above on a bridge specially built to carry The Ridgeway and it's soon forgotten.

Looking towards Ivinghoe Beacon from Pitstone Hill

History

There's plenty of historical interest to explore close to the route you follow in this section.

For those interested in prehistoric sites, there are long and round barrows, Iron Age forts, and sections of Grim's Ditch to seek out. The oldest barrow, a New Stone Age long barrow at least 4000 years old, is located on Whiteleaf Hill just a stone's throw from the Cross cut in the chalk of the north facing slope. For those skilled at finding them, Bronze Age round barrows dating roughly from 2000 to 750 BC, exist in many places with the most obvious situated just to the north of the path at the bottom of the slope up to Ivinghoe Beacon.

And once you reach your journey's end at the top of Beacon Hill itself, there's an Iron Age fort to greet you. Earlier you will have skirted the edge of a similar fort on Pulpit Hill north of the small village of Lower Cadsden. On Pitstone Hill as you emerge from the woodland of Aldbury Nowers, you walk for a while on the edge of a section of Grim's Ditch. This one, unlike that in section 3, is in the open surrounded by chalk grassland.

There is also ample evidence of Man's more recent activities. There are chalk figures cut into the side of the hills at Bledlow and Whiteleaf, a memorial to the men of Buckinghamshire who died during the Boer War in South Africa at the turn of this century atop the highest point in the Chilterns, Coombe Hill, and two important country houses, Chequers, the Prime Minister's country residence, and Tring Park close to the Trail.

Maps

Landranger maps	165	Aylesbury and Leighton Buzzard
Explorer maps	181	Chiltern Hills North
Pathfinder maps	1117 (SU60/70)	Thame
	1118 (SU80/90)	Chesham and Wendover
	1094 (SP81/91)	Aylesbury and Tring

Public Transport Information

National Rail all sections   24 hours a day 0345 484950
www.railtrack.co.uk

Oxfordshire County Council   01865 810405
Buckinghamshire County Council   0345 382000
Hertfordshire County Council   0345 244344

Car Parking

The following are places close to or on The Ridgeway, other than villages or towns, with parking for vehicles - at some only for a few. Unfortunately theft from vehicles parked in the countryside does occasionally occur so please leave valuables at home.

Place	Map Grid Reference
On Ridgeway on east side of minor road to Bledlow Ridge 1 km south of Chinnor	SP 761003
Princes Risborough public car park	SP 810034
Whiteleaf car park, 1 km east of Princes Risborough Turn right off A4010 at Monks Risborough and car park is on left at top of escarpment	SP 824036
National Trust car park for Coombe Hill, 2 km southwest of Wendover. From Wendover travel west on minor road to Princes Risborough. Take first left then first left again. At top of hill car park is on left.	SP 852062
Wendover public car park	SP 868077
Pitstone Hill car park east of Tring. From sharp bend on B488, 1 km southeast of Ivinghoe, take minor road signposted Aldbury. Car park is on right after 1 km.	SP 955149
National Trust car park for Ivinghoe Beacon, on the left of minor road to Ringshall, 1 km south off the B489.	SP 962162

Taxis

Place	Name	Telephone Number
Chinnor	Chinnor Cabs	01844 353637
Bledlow Ridge	Ridge Rentals	01494 481568
Princes Risborough	B & V Taxis	01844 342079
	Village Cars	01844 342551
	Red Line Car Hire	01844 343736
Longwick	Witcher's Chauffeur Service	01844 344239/040 355 1498
High Wycombe	0001 Wycombe Taxis	01494 463360
	Tiger Taxis	01494 461111
	A Cars	01494 523344
	A1 Taxi Service	01494 441000
Wendover	Chilton Taxis	01296 624838
Wigginton	Barrington Taxis	01442 823263
Aylesbury	001 Emergency Cabs	01296 339999
	A1 Taxis	01296 425555/489777
	A to B Taxis	01296 399299
	Eagles Cars	01296 422121
Tring	Bev's Cars	01442 824105
	M&H Car Hire	01442 825795
	Mike's Private Hire	01442 826161

Toilets

Place	Map Grid Reference
Princes Risborough (Horn Mill Car Park)	SP 809033
Wendover (Library Car Park)	SP 868078

Police

Oxfordshire and Buckinghamshire	01865 846000
Hertfordshire	01707 354200

Hospitals

Place	Telephone Number	Address
Aylesbury	01296 315000	Stoke Mandeville Hospital, Mandeville Road, Aylesbury.

Vets

Place	Name	Telephone Number
Princes Risborough	Sprinz and Nash	01844 345655
Wendover	Wendover Heights	01296 623439
Tring	Springwell	01442 822151

Farriers

Place	Name	Telephone Number
Aylesbury	A E Speller	01296 393896/0958 993557

Saddlers

Place	Name	Telephone Number
Chartridge (near The Lee)	Chris Gohl	01494 837138
Wendover	Summerfield's	01296 622081
Westcott	Balance	01296 658333
Aylesbury	Dennis's	01296 484752

Mountain Bike Hire

Place	Name	Telephone Number
Princes Risborough	Boltons Bikes	01844 345949

Bike Repairs

Place	Name	Telephone Number
Princes Risborough	Boltons Bikes	01844 345949
Aylesbury	Buckingham Bikes	01296 822201
Berkhampsted	Dees Cycles	01442 877447
Dunstable	Dysons Cycles	01582 665533

Tourist Information Centres

★ offers accommodation booking service

Place	Address/Opening Hours
★ Thame (★Visitors to office only)	Market House, North Street, Thame OX9 3HH Tel/fax: 01844 212834 Opening hours: August: Mon-Fri 09:30-17:00, Sat 10:00-16:00, Sun/Bank Hols 10:00-15:00 Rest of year: Mon-Fri 09:30-17:00, Sat 10:00-16:00
Princes Risborough	Tower Court, Horns Lane, Princes Risborough HP27 OAJ Tel: 01844 274795 Fax: 01844 275795 Opening hours: All year: Mon-Fri 09:00-17:00
★ Wendover	Clock Tower, High Street, Wendover HP22 6AA Tel: 01296 696759 Fax: 01296 622460 Opening hours: All year: Mon-Sat 10:00-16:00
Tring	99 Akeman Street, Tring HP23 6AA Tel/Fax: 01442 823347 email: tring@mildram.co.uk Opening hours: All year: Mon-Fri 09:30-15:00, Sat 10:00-13:00
Berkhampsted	c/o Berkhampsted Library, Kings Road, Berkhampsted HP4 3BD Tel: 01438 737333 (ask for Berkhampsted Library) Opening hours: All year: Mon 09:30-17:30, Tue 10:30-20:00, Wed closed, Thu 09:30-20:00, Fri 09:30-17:30, Sat 09:30-16:00
Dunstable	c/o Dunstable Library, Vernon Place, Dunstable LU5 4HA Tel: 01582 471012 Fax: 01582 471290 Opening hours: All year: Mon-Fri 10:00-17:00, Sat 09:30-16:00

Monument on Coombe Hil

LODGE HILL

SP7900 on The Ridgeway

Old Callow Down Farm *closed Nov 2000*

Mrs N E Gee
Old Callow Down Farm, Wigans Lane,
Bledlow Ridge,
HIGH WYCOMBE HP14 4BH
☎ 01844 344416 **Fax:** 01844 344703
Email: oldcallow@aol.com

1 £44.00 (£30.00)

V ◆◆◆ 300m south of Ridgeway

SAUNDERTON

SP7901 1km

 S M T W T F S   S M T W T F S

The Rose and Crown Hotel *Dec 24 - Jan 2*

Mrs H Watson
The Rose and Crown Hotel, Wycombe
Road, Saunderton,
PRINCES RISBOROUGH HP27 9NP
☎ 01844 345299 **Fax:** 01844 343140
Email: rose.crown@btinternet.com
Web: www.btinternet.com/mrose.crown

11 1 £69.95
3 £49.50 (£49.50)
V ★★

View from Lodge Hill

BRADENHAM

SU8297  5km ☎

🍺 |||||||||||| S M T W T F S ✕ ■||||||| S M T W T F S

 YHA Bradenham *phone ahead*

YHA Bradenham, The Village Hall,
Bradenham, HIGH WYCOMBE HP14 4HF
☎ 01494 562929 **Fax:** 01494 564743
Email: bradenham@yha.org.uk

🚫 👫 🚭 ♿ **DRY** 🚲 📮 Dormitory
accommodation £8.75/person

HADDENHAM

SP7408  7.5km ☎

🍺 |||||||||| S M T W T F S ✕ |||||||||| S M T W T F S
✉ |||||||||| S M T W T F S 🧺 |||||||||| S M T W T F S
🫖 |||||||||| S M T W T F S ✂ |||||||||| S M T W T F S
🎁 |||||||||| S M T W T F S

☆ Haddenham Village Museum
(Tel: 01844 290791).

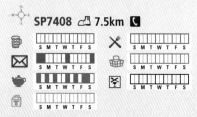

Aylesbury Vale from Coombe Hill

| Cover Point | *all year* |

Mrs P Collins
Cover Point, 19 The Croft, Haddenham,
AYLESBURY HP17 8AS
☎ 01844 290093

🛏 1 £45.00 (£25.00)

V 🔥 🚫 📮 👫 🚭 **DRY** 🚲 🚗
👣 📮 Offers holiday package with
transport to/from daily start/finish points
on Ridgeway

PRINCES RISBOROUGH

SP8003 on The Ridgeway
Market town with a range of services ℹ

| The Black Prince | *all year* |

Mr S Keen
The Black Prince, 86 Wycombe Road,
PRINCES RISBOROUGH HP27 0EN
☎ 01844 345569 **Fax:** 01844 345076

🛏 1 🛏 3 🛏 1 £40.00
🛏 3 £26.50 (£30.00)

🔥 🚫 👫 🚲 👣

WHITELEAF

SP8204 🥾 1km

🍺 |||||||||| S M T W T F S   ✗ |||||||||| S M T W T F S

LOWER CADSDEN

SP8204 🥾 on The Ridgeway

🍺 |||||||||| S M T W T F S   ✗ |||||||||| S M T W T F S

ASKETT

SP8105 🥾 2km

🍺 |||||||||| S M T W T F S   ✗ |||||||||| S M T W T F S

GREAT KIMBLE

SP8206 🥾 1km 📞

🍺 |||||||||| S M T W T F S   ✗ |||||||||| S M T W T F S

BUTLERS CROSS

SP8407 🥾 1km 📞

🍺 |||||||||| S M T W T F S   ✗ |||||||||| S M T W T F S

CHALFONT ST GILES

SU9893 🥾 20km

Town with range of services

Solis Ortu *all year*

Mrs P Crockett
Solis Ortu, Aylesbury Road, Askett,
PRINCES RISBOROUGH HP27 9LY
☎ 01844 344175 **Fax:** 01844 343509
Email: crockett@bucksnet.co.uk

🛏 2 🚿 1 £45.00 (£25.00)

V 🏵 ⓝ 🚻 🚭 🚲 🚗 ♦♦♦

Chequers

Buckinghamshire Chilterns Univ College ▦
closed Oct–May

Ms J Wainwright
Buckinghamshire Chilterns Univ College,
Chalfont Campus, Newland Park,
Gorelands Lane,
CHALFONT ST GILES HP8 4AD
☎ 01494 603064 **Fax:** 01494 603078
Email: conferenceoffice@bcuc.ac.uk
Website: www.cyber-guide.co.uk/
st-peter/buckscollege

🚿 40 £45.00 🚗 40 £30.00 (£45.00)

V 🏵 ⓝ 🚻 ♿ **DRY** 🚲

▦ from £300 per week

WENDOVER

SP8607 🥾 on The Ridgeway

🍺 S M T W T F S   ✗ S M T W T F S

✉ S M T W T F S   🧺 S M T W T F S

🫖 S M T W T F S   🍸 S M T W T F S

🗄 S M T W T F S

📞 ♿ £ Lloyds 🏧 Barclays 🛈

☆ Wendover Woods (Tel: 01296 625825)

Belton House   *closed Xmas*

Mrs E C Condie
Belton House, 26 Chiltern Road,
WENDOVER HP22 6DB
☎ 01296 622351

🛏 1 £30.00 🛌 1 £15.00 (£15.00)

🚭 🔌 ♿ 🚭 DRY 🔪 Breakfast food
provided to prepare in self-catering
kitchen.

Dunsmore Edge   *closed Xmas, New Year*

Mr & Mrs R A Drackford
Dunsmore Edge, London Road,
Wendover, AYLESBURY HP22 6PN
☎ 01296 623080

🛏 2 £39.00 🛌 2 £19.50

V 🔥 🚭 ♿ 🚭 DRY 🚲 🚗 ◆◆◆

The Red Lion Hotel   *all year*

Mrs J Hills
The Red Lion Hotel, 9 High Street,
Wendover, AYLESBURY HP22 6DU
☎ 01296 622266 **Fax:** 01296 625077

🛏 12 🛌 3 🛌 3 £65.00
🛌 2 £55.00 (£55.00)

V 🔥 🚭 👫 DRY 🚲 ★★

Mrs MacDonald's — *closed Xmas*

Mr G MacDonald
Mrs MacDonald's, 46 Lionel Avenue,
Wendover, AYLESBURY HP22 6LP
☎ 01296 623426

🛏 1 £44.00 🛏 2 £22.00 (£22.00)

V
 ◆◆◆

THE LEE

SP9004 ⌂ 3km

Patchwicks — *all year*

Mrs J Syer
Patchwicks, The Lee,
GREAT MISSENDEN HP16 9LZ
☎ 01494 837596

🛏 1 🛏 1 £36.00 (£20.00)

V

ST LEONARDS

SP9107 ⌂ 1.5km

Field Cottage — *all year*

Mrs S Jepson
Field Cottage, St Leonards,
TRING HP23 6NS
☎ 01494 837602

🛏 1 🛏 1 £50.00 (£30.00)

V except Mondays over 12 yrs

◆◆◆◆ Silver Award 2000

WIGGINTON

SP9310 ⌂ on The Ridgeway

Rangers Cottage — *closed Xmas, New Year*

Mrs S Dawson
Rangers Cottage, Tring Park, Wigginton,
TRING HP23 6EB
☎ 01442 890155 **Fax:** 01442 890155

🛏 2 🛏 1 £54.00 (£39.00)

opening 1 April 2000

North of Tring Station

Lodge Hill from the west

RIDGEWAY
FOOTPATH

FOOTPATH
NO CYCLES

Bacombe Hill west of Wendover

TRING

SP9211 ⌁ 2km

Small town with range of services

 ☆ Tring Zoological Museum (Tel: 01442 824181)

ALDBURY

SP9612 ⌁ 1km C

☆ Ashridge Estate (Tel: 01442 842488)

PITSTONE

SP9315 ⌁ 2.5km C

☆ Pitstone Green Farm Museum (Tel: 01582 605464); Pitstone Windmill (Tel: 01582 872303)

IVINGHOE

SP9416 ⌁ 1.5km C

☆ Ford End Watermill (Tel: 01582 600391)

YHA Ivinghoe — *phone ahead*

YHA Ivinghoe, The Old Brewery House,
High Street, Ivinghoe,
LEIGHTON BUZZARD LU7 9EP
☎ 01296 668251 **Fax:** 01296 662903
Email: ivinghoe@yha.org.uk

V ♿ ⬤ ⚥ ⊘ **DRY** ⬲
☒ Dormitory accommodation £9.00/person

EDLESBOROUGH

SP9719 ⌁ 3km C

Ridgeway End — *closed Xmas, New Year*

Mrs J Lloyd
Ridgeway End, 5 Ivinghoe Way,
Edlesborough, DUNSTABLE LU6 2EL
☎ 01525 220405 **Mob:** 0421 027 339
Fax: 01525 220405

 2 🛏 1 🛏 1 £44.00 (£24.00)

V ♿ ⬤ ⚥ ⊘ **DRY** ⬲ 🚗

Index of Places

Aldbury 93
Aldworth 61
Ardington 59
Ashbury 43-44
Askett 89
Aston Rowant 77
Avebury 39
Barbury Castle 40
Benson 73-74
Bishopstone 42-43
Bledlow 77
Blewbury 61
Bradenham 88
Broad Hinton 39
Butlers Cross 89
Chalfont St Giles 89
Chalgrove 76
Cherhill 38
Childrey 56
Chilton 60
Chinnor 77
Chiseldon 41
Cholsey 61
Compton 60
Crowmarsh Gifford 72
East Hendred 59
East Ilsley 60
Edlesborough 93
Faringdon 46
Goring 69
Great Kimble 89
Haddenham 88
Ivinghoe 93
Kingston Lisle 55
Letcombe Regis 56-57
Lewknor 76
Liddington 41
Lockeridge 38

Lodge Hill 87
Lower Cadsden 89
Marlborough 37
Moulsford 61
North Stoke 71
Nuffield 74
Ogbourne St George 40-41
Park Corner 75
Pewsey 37
Pishill 75
Pitstone 93
Postcombe 76
Princes Risborough 88
Saunderton 87
South Stoke 71
Sparsholt 55-56
St Leonards 91
Streatley 62
Swindon 40
Sydenham 77
The Lee 91
Tring 93
Uffington 46
Upton 60
Wallingford 73
Wanborough 41-42
Wantage 58
Watlington 75-76
Wendover 90-91
West Hendred 59
West Ilsley 60
West Overton 38
Whiteleaf 89
Wigginton 91
Winterbourne Bassett 39
Winterbourne Monkton 39
Woolstone 44-45
Wroughton 40